P9-CCM-577

50 Signs of the Times

and the Second Coming

By
David J. Ridges

CFI

Springville, Utah

Copyright © 2004 David J. Ridges

All Rights Reserved.

No part of this book may be reproduced in any form whatsoever, whether by graphic, visual, electronic, film, microfilm, tape recording, or any other means, without prior written permission of the author, except in the case of brief passages embodied in critical reviews and articles.

ISBN: 1-55517-718-2
e.1

Published by Bonneville Books
Imprint of Cedar Fort Inc.
www.cedarfort.com

Distributed by:

Cover design by Nicole Cunningham
Cover design © 2004 by Lyle Mortimer

Printed in the United States of America
10 9 8 7 6 5 4 3 2 1

Printed on acid-free paper

Library of Congress Control Number: 2003112603

50 Signs of the Times
and the Second Coming

Books
by David J. Ridges

The *Gospel Studies Series:*

- Volume 1: Isaiah Made Easier
- Volume 2: The New Testament Made Easier, Part 1
- Volume 3: The New Testament Made Easier, Part 2

Upcoming volumes in the *Gospel Studies Series*:

- Your Study of The Book of Mormon Made Easier (2004)
- Your Study of The Doctrine & Covenants Made Easier (2005)
- Your Study of The Pearl of Great Price Made Easier (2006)
- The Old Testament Made Easier—Selections from the Old Testament (2006)

Additional titles by David J. Ridges:

- The Proclamation on the Family: The Word of the Lord on More Than 30 Current Issues
- From Premortality to Exaltation: Doctrinal Details of the Plan of Salvation (2004)

Watch for these titles to also become available through Cedar Fort as e-books and on CD.

FOREWORD

There is widespread interest in the signs of the times among members of the Church as well as among Christians in general. "Signs of the times" is a phrase which refers to prophecies given by the Lord's prophets throughout the history of the world which refer to events which will take place leading up to the Savior's Second Coming. As the faithful study these signs, they become more aware that it is a marvelous and exciting day to be alive! Prophecies are being fulfilled on every side! Testimonies are thus strengthened and assurance is given that the scriptures are true. This is the positive approach which we will use in this book as we view these signs.

We will look at 50 signs of the times. The format is concise and makes it easy for the reader to see these signs of the times at a glance and get more information about them as desired. For our purposes, we have assigned most of the signs to one of the three following categories:

Three general categories:
1. Fulfilled
2. Being Fulfilled
3. Yet Future

With some, though, as you will see, we have simply assigned a question mark **(?)** because we don't know which of the categories they belong in. With many of the signs of the times which we will consider, the lines between these categories will be rather clear. But with some, the lines will be blurry, and, in fact, the fulfillment of some signs could involve two categories and sometimes all three. It is particularly interesting to look at the signs which are yet future.

The Savior will come. He will be right on time. It is the

privilege of those who study the scriptures and heed the words of the prophets, ancient and modern, to be informed. They are "the children of light" (D&C 106:5) and will be alerted by the signs of the times as His coming draws near. Because of the fulfillment of these prophecies, they can look forward to it with increased testimony and will not be caught off guard when He comes.

An especially deep expression of appreciation goes to my wife, Janette, who has encouraged and helped throughout the writing of this work.

David J. Ridges

TABLE OF CONTENTS

CHAPTER 1

THE LAST DAYS, AN EXCITING TIME TO LIVE

The Second Coming of Christ is mentioned over 1,500 times in the Old Testament and some 300 times in the New Testament. It is a much-anticipated event in our day. In this book, we will formally consider 50 "signs of the times". Signs of the times are prophecies which the Lord has given His prophets, recorded throughout ancient and modern scripture, which are designed to alert the faithful in the last days that the coming of the Lord is near. They are designed to strengthen testimonies and provide encouragement and confidence in the hearts of believers in a day when many no longer even believe in God. Every one of these prophecies will be fulfilled. As we prepare to discuss the 50 signs of the times selected for consideration in this book, we will first look at a number of cautions and observations concerning this subject. Then we will list and look at the 50 signs themselves. Finally, we will take a quick look at what will actually happen when the Savior comes.

Several years ago, one of my students raised her hand in class and asked, "Wouldn't it be nice if our modern prophets had real revelations, like ancient prophets did in the scriptures?" It was a bit difficult to stifle a grin as I responded to her question. Of course, the class discussion which resulted led to the definite conclusion that they do! And one of the most important revelations to the Church in these last days, coming through President Gordon B. Hinckley, which was pointed out in that class, is that these last days are a wonderful time to be alive! How many times have you heard him say, in one way or another, that this is a great time to be alive? How many talks of his have you heard in which he said, in effect, "What a wonderful day to be alive!" For example, in the Saturday morning session of General Conference, October, 5, 2001, President Hinckley said:

> *"I do not know what we did in the preexistence to merit the wonderful blessings we enjoy. We have come to earth in this great season in the long history of mankind. It is a marvelous age, the best of all. As we reflect on the plodding course of mankind, from the time of our first parents, we cannot help feeling grateful." (November 2001 Ensign.)*

To some, at first, this may not seem particularly spectacular. But it is! One of the signs of the times which is given in many places, is that in the last days there will be much of gloom and doom and much of fear, discouragement and despair. For instance, Luke describes one of the prevailing conditions in the last days, before the Savior's coming, as follows (bold used for emphasis):

> 25 And there shall be signs in the sun, and in the moon, and in the stars; and upon the earth distress of nations, with perplexity; the sea and the waves roaring;
>
> 26 **Men's hearts failing them for fear,** and for looking after those things which are coming on the earth: for the powers of heaven shall be shaken.
> —Luke 21:25-26

President Hinckley's prophetic counsel reminds us to avoid getting caught up in the prevailing pessimism and fatalism which permeates much of the thinking of our day. The word "hearts" in verse 26, above, as used in the scriptures, usually means "courage, hope, confidence etc." "Failing" means "to run out of." Thus, the phrase "Men's hearts failing them for fear" can mean that there will be much of depression in the final times before the Second Coming. This sign of the times is very obviously coming to pass. And it is our great blessing and privilege to follow the counsel of President Hinckley and, with the help of the Holy Ghost, do all we can to avoid this plague, including serving one another which brings the spirit of peace and optimism.

President Hinckley is a wonderful prophet to follow. He exudes optimism and has a delightful sense of humor. At a multi-stake regional conference some years ago which I attended, during the Saturday priesthood leadership session, President Hinckley kept the priesthood brethren there laughing for a solid 45 minutes. During a snack break part way through that meeting, a fellow priesthood leader came up to me, his eyes still wide with wonder, and exclaimed, "I didn't know that a prophet was allowed by the Lord to be funny. I mean, President Hinckley is really funny! He's good!" And so he is. What a great example of happiness and hope and optimism from the Lord's mouthpiece!

These last days before the Savior's return are indeed an exciting time to be alive. There is so much of fascinating technology. There are so many advances in medical science and practice. The Church is expanding and the gospel is spreading throughout the world as never before. Unprecedented communications technology allows us to keep in touch with friends and loved ones no matter where we go or serve. We can visit exotic and faraway places without ever leaving home. Although Satan and his evil allies use such advances to further their evil schemes, if we follow President Hinckley's advice we will emphasize the positives and do our best to limit the negatives and thus appreciate and enjoy the vast blessings of living in the last days.

Since Adam's Fall, man has been concerned w/ time

CHAPTER 2

SOME CAUTIONS AND OBSERVATIONS

Before we deal with fifty specific signs of the times, beginning in chapter 3, some cautions and observations are in order.

First of all, there is no question as to the fact that Satan is intensifying his efforts to deceive us in the last days. Revelation 12:12 gives us an insight as to why this is the case (bold added for emphasis):

> 12 "Therefore rejoice, ye heavens, and ye that dwell in them. Woe to the inhabiters of the earth and of the sea! for the devil is come down unto you, having great wrath, **because he knoweth that he hath but a short time.**"

Even though it could still be many years before the Savior comes, Satan's time is very limited. We learn from D&C 77:6 that the earth has a total of 7,000 years for its "temporal" existence. "Temporal" has to do with time, and "time" has had mortal significance for us since the fall of Adam and will continue to have such meaning until the earth becomes a celestial planet upon which time will no longer be significant because its celestial inhabitants will be in eternity. We are aware that the earth has already used up roughly 6,000 years of its allotted 7,000 "temporal" years, and we know that the Millennium will require 1,000 years. Therefore, Satan has very little time remaining. No wonder he is mounting such an intense last-minute campaign to do as much damage as possible before his evil kingdom falls at the Second Coming! He indeed knows that he has "but a short time!"

It may be worthwhile at this point to look at a few of Lucifer's cunning and widespread deceptions as he intensifies his efforts to lead us astray in these last days. Certainly, one of his angles of attack is to do away with decent heroes. For instance, it is sad to note how many writers and historians have joined in the effort to "dethrone" our founding fathers as heroes for residents of the United States of America and others. These writers and historians seem to want to rewrite history and superimpose their own lack of virtue and character on our national heroes, perhaps as a means of justifying their own departure from God's ways.

When we encounter such "mud-slinging" upon the founders of our constitution, we would do well to study what the Lord says about these great individuals. There is safety and stability in sticking with God on such issues. Staying close to the revelations of God in this matter of our founding fathers will help us remain sound in our thinking and retain honorable heroes. In D&C 101:77-80, the Lord says (bold added for emphasis):

77 According to the laws and constitution of the people, which I have suffered to be established, and should be maintained for the rights and protection of all flesh, according to just and holy principles;

78 That every man may act in doctrine and principle pertaining to futurity, according to the moral agency which I have given unto him, that every man may be accountable for his own sins in the day of judgment.

79 Therefore, it is not right that any man should be in bondage one to another.

80 And for this purpose have I established the Constitution of this land, by the hands of **wise men whom I raised up unto this very purpose**, and redeemed the land by the shedding of blood.

Thus we see that the framers of our Constitution were great premortal spirits who were sent to this earth by the Lord to set up the Constitution of the United States. In fact, almost all of these great men now are members of the Church. How did that happen? President Wilford Woodruff tells us:

> "I will here say, before closing, that two weeks before I left St. George, the spirits of the dead gathered around me, wanting to know why we did not redeem them. Said they, 'You have had the use of the Endowment House for a number of years, and yet nothing has ever been done for us. We laid the foundation of the government you now enjoy, and we never apostatized from it, but we remained true to it and were faithful to God.' These were the signers of the Declaration of Independence, and they waited on me for two days and two nights. I thought it very singular, that notwithstanding so much work had been done, and yet nothing had been done for them. The thought never entered my heart, from the fact, I suppose, that heretofore our minds were reaching after our more immediate friends and relatives. I straightway went into the baptismal font and called upon brother McCallister to baptize me for the signers of the Declaration of Independence, and fifty other eminent men, making one hundred in all, including John Wesley, Columbus, and others; I then baptized him for every President of the United States, except three; and when their cause is just, somebody will do the work for them." (Journal of Discourses, 26 vols. [London: Latter-day Saints' Book Depot, 1854-1886], 19: 229 - 230.)

It is significant that these great men were permitted by the Lord to come to His holy temple and personally request that their temple work be done. It is a fitting finale to their dedicating their all to the cause of freedom during their mortal lives. To say that we all benefit from their sacrifices in our behalf is an understatement.

It is interesting to note that among the men who appeared were Daniel Webster, Henry Clay, and Benito Juarez who was the "Abraham Lincoln" of Mexico. Also, after Brother McCallister had baptized Wilford Woodruff for those one hundred men, Sister Lucy Bigelow Young was then baptized for 70 prominent women, including Martha Washington and Elizabeth Barrett Browning. For more information on these baptisms, see Cowen, *Temples to Dot the Earth*, pp 79-80.

Another all-out effort on Lucifer's part to deceive and destroy in our last days is his evil effort to pit men against women. This is an obvious and overt attempt at the destruction of families, which, according to "The Family: A Proclamation To The World" given September 23, 1995, is the "fundamental unit of society". Pitting men against women and women against men destroys unity and teamwork. It destroys the very finest of feelings and relationships. The debate rages on as to who is most important, man or woman. The battle for equality continues and often turns into a battle for supremacy. And what is the truth? Are men and women truly equal? This is a place where correct doctrine comes to the rescue. In fact, one of the ways to avoid deception and gloom and trouble in the last days is to understand correct doctrine and conform our behaviors and thought processes to it. It brings peace.

So, what has the Lord said about the equality of men and women? What is correct doctrine? One of the most recent revelations from the Lord on this matter came in the proclamation on the family as mentioned above. Given by the First Presidency and the Council of the Twelve Apostles, on September 23, 1995, the word of the Lord is (bold added for emphasis): "...fathers and mothers are obligated to help one another as **equal partners.**" This is correct doctrine. Men and women are to be equal partners now as well as in eternity. If our attitudes and behaviors do not reflect this eternal truth, then we need to change, repent, and conform genuinely to the truth.

Please note that this eternal truth about the equality of men and women is taught very clearly in D&C 132:19-20. Here the

Lord says (bold added for emphasis):

> 19 And again, verily I say unto you, **if a man marry a wife** by my word, which is my law, and by the new and everlasting covenant, and it is sealed unto them by the Holy Spirit of promise, by him who is anointed, unto whom I have appointed this power and the keys of this priesthood; and it shall be said unto **them**—Ye shall come forth in the first resurrection; and if it be after the first resurrection, in the next resurrection; and shall inherit thrones, kingdoms, principalities, and powers, dominions, all heights and depths—then shall it be written in the Lamb's Book of Life, that he shall commit no murder whereby to shed innocent blood, and if ye abide in my covenant, and commit no murder whereby to shed innocent blood, it shall be done unto **them** in all things whatsoever my servant hath put upon **them**, in time, and through all eternity; and shall be of full force when **they** are out of the world; and **they** shall pass by the angels, and the gods, which are set there, to **their** exaltation and glory in all things, as hath been sealed upon **their** heads, which glory shall be a fulness and a continuation of the seeds forever and ever.
>
> 20 Then shall **they** be gods, because **they** have no end; therefore shall **they** be from everlasting to everlasting, because **they** continue; then shall **they** be above all, because all things are subject unto **them**. Then shall **they** be gods, because they have all power, and the angels are subject unto **them**.

If anyone has trouble still in understanding this truth, the teaching of Bruce R. McConkie can help. He said:

> *"If righteous men have power through the gospel and its crowning ordinance of celestial marriage to become kings and priests to rule in exaltation forever, it follows that the women*

by their side (without whom they cannot attain exaltation) will be queens and priestesses. (Revelation 1:6; 5:10.) Exaltation grows out of the eternal union of a man and his wife. Of those whose marriage endures in eternity, the Lord says, 'Then shall they be gods.' (D&C 132:20.); that is, each of them, the man and the woman, will be a god. As such they will rule over their dominions forever." (McConkie, Mormon Doctrine, *second edition, Salt Lake City: Bookcraft, 1966, page 613.)*

Understanding correct doctrine has great power to change and mold thought processes and behaviors. Thus, understanding correct doctrine is essential for our progression toward becoming like our Father in Heaven. In Alma, chapters 39-42, Alma skillfully used correct doctrines to help Corianton change his thinking on vital issues. Elder Boyd K. Packer said:

"True doctrine, understood, changes attitudes and behavior. The study of the doctrines of the gospel will improve behavior quicker than a study of behavior will improve behavior." (General Conference, October 1986.)

Understanding correct doctrine on the equality of men and women can keep us from getting caught up in Satan's deceptions on this very significant issue. Indeed, understanding and applying correct doctrine blesses our lives with respect to many other matters calculated by the adversary to keep things stirred up so that peace and righteous satisfaction elude many during the final scenes before the Lord's coming.

AVOID USING THE SIGNS OF THE TIMES TO FRIGHTEN OR SPREAD PANIC.

Unfortunately, whether intentional or not, many who teach and discuss the signs of the times seem to end up causing fear and panic in the hearts and minds of their listeners. Let's see what the Savior says about this. In Joseph Smith–Matthew, chapter one, in our Pearl of Great Price, the Master answers questions asked by His disciples concerning the times which will precede the Second Coming. As His disciples listened intently, it appears that fear and concern entered their hearts. In response, Jesus said (bold added for emphasis):

> 23 Behold, I speak these things unto you for the elect's sake; and you also shall hear of wars, and rumors of wars; **see that ye be not troubled**, for all I have told you must come to pass; but the end is not yet.

It is very significant that the Savior instructed His loyal followers not to use the signs of the times to promote fear and trouble in their own hearts. We should follow that counsel too. Christ continues in that chapter to emphasize the value of preparation as well as the fact that the signs of the times are designed to strengthen people's testimonies. In JS–Matt., chapter one, He continued (bold added for emphasis):

> 35 Although, the days will come, that heaven and earth shall pass away; yet **my words** shall not pass away, but **all shall be fulfilled**.

> 37 And **whoso treasureth up my word, shall not be deceived**, for the Son of Man shall come, and he shall send his angels before him with the great sound of a trumpet, and they shall gather together the remainder of his elect from the four winds, from one end of heaven to the other.

> 39 So likewise, mine elect, **when they shall see all these things, they shall know** that he is near, even at the doors;

Thus, the Savior emphasizes that the signs of the times are given to help faithful saints "know" that His coming is close. This "knowing" which comes from obvious, observable fulfillment of prophecy is a powerful testimony strengthener. These signs, then, are given to inform, to bear witness to us, and to reassure.

Most people claim that there is no such thing as proof that God exists. I beg to differ. I believe that the signs of the times fit the so-called "scientific method." In my training in physics and other science classes in school and university classes, we were taught the "scientific method." Essentially, this method consists of forming a hypothesis, then observing things to see if the hypothesis turns out to be credible or false. If, over time and with continued observation, sufficient positive evidence turns up, the hypothesis is changed to a theory. If enough supporting evidence continues to be gathered, it can be considered to be proof or truth, and many scientific advancements and products are made, based upon it. So also with the signs of the times. It is as if the Lord were saying: "In the last days, there will be many who do not believe in God. Therefore, I will place many prophecies in the scriptures which will be fulfilled prior to the Second Coming. There will be so many of these 'signs of the times' that anyone who is honest in heart will be able to consider them as proof that I do exist." In the world of science, so many "coincidences" or "lucky guesses" would not be considered "coincidences." The signs of the times are not coincidences. They are obvious proof that God exists and that His Son will come again.

President Gordon B. Hinckley gave the following counsel about fear in the last days (bold added for emphasis):

> *"Are these perilous times? They are. But* **there is no need to fear.** *We can have peace in our hearts and peace in our homes. We can be an influence for good in this world, every one of us." (General Conference, October 2001.)*

THE "MARK OF THE BEAST"

One of the most often quoted scriptural references used inappropriately in our day to spread fear among people is

Revelation, chapter 13. In this tremendous chapter, John the Revelator warns against many of Satan's ploys and deceptions in the last days. Among other things, John refers to the "mark of the beast." Unfortunately, many people misread verses 15 through 17 and come to believe that all people in the last days will come under the domination and evil control of the "beast."

According to the heading for chapter 13, the "beasts" referred to in the chapter "represent degenerate earthly kingdoms controlled by Satan." Let's look at Revelation 13:15-17, and then discuss it. We will bold words and phrases which seem to lead to misinterpretation.

> 15 And he had power to give life unto the image of the beast, that the image of the beast should both speak, and cause that as many **as would not worship the image of the beast should be killed.**
> 16 And he causeth **all**, both small and great, rich and poor, free and bond, to **receive a mark in their right hand, or in their foreheads:**
> 17 And that **no man** might buy or sell, save he that had the mark, or the name of the beast, or the number of his name.

If we were to use these verses exclusively, and pay attention especially to the bolded portions of the verses above, we would, as do many others, conclude that Satan will gain such a stranglehold and such awful power in the final days before the Second Coming that everyone including the righteous saints will ultimately come under his power and control. This is not the case. The problem with this approach, which leads to gloom and despair and hopelessness, is that it ignores other verses in the Book of Revelation. It also ignores President Hinckley's counsel to look at the bright side. If we joined others in their misinterpretation of the above verses, there would be no bright side.

Other verses within the Book of Revelation itself show that everyone does not come under the grasp and power of the "beast." Some of these verses follow (bold added for emphasis):

Revelation 14:9.

> 9 And the third angel followed them, saying with a loud voice, **If** any man worship the beast and his image, and receive his mark in his forehead, or in his hand,

Revelation 20:4.

> 4 And I saw thrones, and they sat upon them, and judgment was given unto them: and I saw the souls of them that were beheaded for the witness of Jesus, and for the word of God, and which **had not worshipped the beast**, neither his image, **neither had received his mark upon their foreheads,** or in their hands; and they lived and reigned with Christ a thousand years.

Revelation 22:3-4.

> 3 And there shall be no more curse: but the throne of God and of **the Lamb** shall be in it; and **his servants shall serve him:**
> 4 And they shall see his face; and **his name shall be in their foreheads.**

"Context" is key in interpreting and understanding verses such as Revelation 13:15-17. When seen in the context of the whole Book of Revelation, indeed, in the context of the whole standard works and the words of modern prophets, such misunderstanding and discomfort attending chapter 13 is remedied. We conclude that only the wicked and those who foolishly ignore the counsel of the prophets to live the gospel, to live within their means, etc. will fall under the control of the "beast" in the last days before the coming of the Lord. This, indeed, is one of the signs of the times and is being fulfilled rather dramatically as we speak.

An interesting question comes up as we study these verses. What does "forehead" symbolize? Answer. In Jewish culture, forehead symbolizes loyalty. Thus, in Revelation 14:1, we see 144,000 who are loyal to the Father (bold added for emphasis):

> 1 And I looked, and, lo, a Lamb stood on the mount Sion, and with him an hundred forty and four thousand, having his **Father's name written in their foreheads.**

In Revelation 7:2-3, we see servants who are loyal to God (bold added for emphasis):

> 2 And I saw another angel ascending from the east, having the seal of the living God: and he cried with a loud voice to the four angels, to whom it was given to hurt the earth and the sea,
> 3 Saying, Hurt not the earth, neither the sea, nor the trees, **till we have sealed the servants of our God in their foreheads.**

Simply put, symbolically, those who are loyal to wickedness, financial greed, etc. are depicted as having the mark of the beast on their foreheads. Whereas, those who are loyal to God and to righteousness are depicted in Jewish cultural symbolism as having the name of God on their foreheads. A similar image is found in Alma 5:14, where the righteous are seen as having the image of Christ in their countenance (bold added for emphasis). This, of course, is literal:

> 14 And now behold, I ask of you, my brethren of the church, have ye spiritually been born of God? Have ye received **his image in your countenances?** Have ye experienced this mighty change in your hearts?

In conclusion, those who insist on taking Revelation 13:15-17 out of context and misinterpreting it, come up with some rather fascinating and widespread false rumors. For instance, many people have come to believe that the "mark of the beast in their foreheads" will turn out to be a bar code, tattooed upon people's foreheads in the last days. And those who do not join in corrupt financial institutions, controlled by secret combinations, and thus qualify to have such a bar code tattooed on their foreheads, will not be allowed to "buy or sell" (Revelation 13:17,) and will perish.

Another variation of the "mark of the beast" rumor is the idea that people who desire to buy and sell in the last days will have a computer chip implanted in their right hand or forehead or whatever. Without this chip, they will perish. In earlier but still recent days, plastic credit cards were considered by some to represent the mark of the beast.

Such rumors do little to help and much to harm. Let us remain true to God and, as a result see the wisdom of having the name of God, in effect, "engraved" upon our features and our souls.

THE EXACT TIMING OF THE SECOND COMING.

The scriptures are very clear in explaining that no one knows the exact timing of the Second Coming of the Savior. Two references are as follows (bold added for emphasis):

Matthew 24:36.

> 36 But of **that day and hour knoweth *no man*,** no, **not the angels** of heaven, but **my Father only.**

Mark 13:32.

> 32 But of that day and that hour knoweth no man, no, not the angels which are in heaven, **neither the Son,** but the Father.

In spite of such scriptures as above quoted, some people still insist on trying to pin down the timing of the Second Coming. For instance, some have been heard to say that even though we can't know the day and hour, we can know the month and year. Some make elaborate calculations, based on personal interpretation of scriptures combined with the statements of prophets to narrow down the timing. When others refuse to accept their calculations as being inspired, they respond by saying that those who are truly in tune with the Spirit will gain a witness that what they claim is true. Still others claim that our prophets and Apostles today do indeed know the exact day and hour, but have been instructed not to tell us.

Elder M. Russell Ballard, of the Quorum of the Twelve, spoke to a BYU devotional audience in the Marriott Center about the last days and signs of the times, on March 12, 1996. He said (bold added for emphasis):

> *"Now with the Lord's help I would like to speak to you about a subject that is on a lot of people's minds.* ***My intention is not to alarm or to frighten,*** *but to discuss the* ***significant and interesting times in which we are now living,*** *to consider some of the events and circumstances we can anticipate in the future and to suggest a few things we can all do to fortify ourselves and our families for the challenges and trials that will surely come into all of our lives at one time or another." Elder Ballard continued, reading from Matthew 24:3-7, reading and commenting, and then paused, saying "I want to pause here for a moment and suggest to you, if you haven't been aware, that some of these things seem to be occurring with ever-increasing regularity. If you measured the natural disasters that have occurred in the world during the last 10 years and plotted that year-by-year, you would see an acceleration. The earth is rumbling, and earthquakes are occurring in 'divers places.' Human nature being what it is, we don't normally pay much attention to these natural phenomena until they happen close to where we are living. But when we contemplate what has happened during the past decade, not only with earthquakes but also with regards to hurricanes, floods, tornadoes, volcanic eruptions, and the like, you would see an accelerating pattern.*

*So, can we use this scientific data to extrapolate that the Second Coming is likely to occur during the next few years, or the next decade, or the next century? Not really. I am called as one of the apostles to be a special witness of Christ in these exciting, trying times, and **I do not know when He is going to come again**. As far as I know, none of my brethren in the Council of the Twelve or even in the First Presidency knows. And I would humbly suggest to you, my young brothers and sisters, that **if we do not know, then nobody knows**, no matter how compelling their arguments or how reasonable their calculations."*

Some years ago, at the conclusion of a Know Your Religion lecture which I gave on the signs of the times, an elderly brother came up to the stand and corrected me by saying, in effect, that Matthew 24:36 ("But of that day and hour knoweth no man...") does not apply to the First Presidency and the Twelve and thus, those Brethren do know. He went on to quote Amos 3:7 which says:

7 Surely the Lord GOD will do nothing, but he revealeth his secret unto his servants the prophets.

He was well-intentioned, and when I quoted Elder Ballard's statement to him, quoted above, he thanked me, saying "I didn't realize Elder Ballard had said that."

As far as I am concerned, such thinking that the Brethren do know the day and even the hour is neither evil nor sinful. It merely expresses a sincere testimony that the Brethren are guided and directed by the Lord. But it could cause trouble and become apostasy if pushed as a "gospel hobby" or if preached as doctrine. It may even be that the Lord will tell the Brethren just before He comes, or it may be that it will pleasantly surprise them. We simply don't know. In fact, in Mark 13:32 as quoted previously, the Savior seems to emphasize "neither the Son, but the Father." We are wise to stick tightly to the scriptures on this one. It is even interesting to note that Revelation 15:15, if we understand it correctly, reinforces the thought that the Father will tell the Son when it is time for the Second Coming. In this verse, John the Revelator describes seeing an angel come out of the temple (where the Father rules upon his throne of power–see Revelation 7:15) with a message from the Father. The angel instructs the Savior that it is "harvest" time, or in other words, time for the Second Coming. As stated above, we are wise to stick closely to the scriptures and avoid speculation.

DO NOT PUT YOUR LIFE ON HOLD, BECAUSE OF THE CLOSENESS OF THE SECOND COMING.

Some years ago, a member came into my office and expressed concern that her husband, a faithful high priest, had decided that since the Savior's coming is getting so close, they would no longer put savings into their account nor contribute toward their retirement plan with their employer. His thinking was that since the Millennium would obviously be starting soon, they would no longer need money, so he wanted to use their savings and retirement funds now for a boat and other things to go along with it. Such thinking is obviously way off the mark!

Occasionally, over the years, students have indicated that they are not sure that it is necessary for them to be pursuing any further education, since the Second Coming is getting so close, and thus their financial needs will all be taken care of as the Millennium arrives. That thinking is also way off base. This is a church which constantly emphasizes preparation for emergencies and long-term preparation for the future. Our prophets encourage education. Simply following the Brethren does away with any notion of putting life on hold because of the proximity of the Second Coming.

It is interesting to note that in the Book of Mormon, Mosiah 3:5, King Benjamin tells his people that the time "is not far distant" when the Savior will be born. "Not far distant," in this case, turns out to be 124 years. The Lord's expression of time is not necessarily the same as ours. Thus, we realize, based on the rapidly fulfilling signs of the times all around us, that the coming of Christ is indeed getting close. However, "getting close" could still mean many, many years. Or, it could mean "just around the corner." Neither of these statements helps to really pin it down. Therefore, we are left to decide which of the groups of "five virgins" we want to be like, the five wise or the five foolish. Both groups started out with oil in their lamps (see Matthew 25:8, footnote a) but the five wise took extra oil in containers along with their lamps (see verses 3 and 4). For both groups, it took longer than they expected for the Bridegroom (Christ) to come (see verse 5) and so they slept while He "tarried," meaning that life went on normally right up until the Bridegroom came. The point we are making here is that, in the parable, it took longer than expected for the Bridegroom to come. Therefore, we would be foolish to put our lives on hold while waiting for the Lord's arrival.

WILL EVERYONE BE CAUGHT OFF GUARD, AS IN THE SCRIPTURAL "THIEF IN THE NIGHT" IMAGERY?

In D&C 106:4-5 we find that not everyone will be caught off guard by the Second Coming, rather, those who are caught up in the ways of the world (bold added for emphasis).

> 4 And again, verily I say unto you, the coming of the Lord draweth nigh, and **it overtaketh the world as a thief in the night—**
> 5 Therefore, gird up your loins, that you may be the **children of light, and that day shall not overtake you as a thief.**

The phrase "the world" as used in verse 4, above, means the worldly, the wicked, the foolish etc., who ignore the scriptures and the words of the prophets and thus, like the people in the days of Noah, are caught off guard by the prophesied destructions. On the other hand, the "children of light" have the light of the gospel and are aware of the signs of the times. Thus, they know that the Second Coming is getting close, and when it actually happens, they are not surprised. The Parable of the Fig Tree, as given in Joseph Smith–Matthew 1:38-40, confirms this as follows (bold added for emphasis):

> 38 Now learn a parable of the fig-tree—When its branches are yet tender, and it begins to put forth leaves, **you know that summer is nigh at hand;**
> 39 So likewise, mine elect, when they shall see all these things, **they shall know that he is near, even at the doors;**
> 40 But of that day, and hour, no one knoweth; no, not the angels of God in heaven, but my Father only.

AVOID TRYING TO DEVELOP AN EXACT SEQUENCE FOR THE FINAL SIGNS OF THE TIMES.

It is rather fascinating to view the signs of the times as a general sequence of events leading up to the actual Coming of the Lord. However, it is wise to avoid attempting to develop an exact sequence for the final few events before the Second Coming. It seems that the Lord does not want us to know the exact sequence of these final fulfillments of prophecy.

For instance, by reading a few scripture references, including Zechariah 14:1-9, which deals with the appearance of the Savior to the Jews in Jerusalem (when the Mount of Olives splits open), one might begin to think that the last days appearance of Christ in battle-torn Jerusalem would signal His immediate coming to the rest of the world. These verses in Zechariah are as follows (bold added for emphasis):

Zechariah 14:1-9.

1 Behold, **the day of the LORD cometh**, and thy spoil shall be divided in the midst of thee.

2 For I will gather **all nations against Jerusalem** to battle; and **the city shall be taken,** and the houses rifled, and the women ravished; and half of the city shall go forth into captivity, and the residue of the people shall not be cut off from the city.

3 **Then shall the LORD go forth, and fight against those nations, as when he fought in the day of battle.**

4 ¶ And **his feet shall stand in that day upon the mount of Olives**, which is before Jerusalem on the east, and the mount of Olives shall cleave in the midst thereof toward the east and toward the west, and there shall be a very great valley; and half of the mountain shall remove toward the north, and half of it toward the south.

5 And ye shall flee to the valley of the mountains; for the valley of the mountains shall reach unto Azal: yea, ye shall flee, like as ye fled from before the earthquake in the days of Uzziah king of Judah: and **the LORD my God shall come, and all the saints with thee.**

6 And it shall come to pass in that day, *that* the light shall not be clear, *nor* dark:

7 But it shall be one day which shall be known to the LORD, not day, nor night: but it shall come to pass, *that* at evening time it shall be light.

8 And it shall be in that day, *that* living waters shall go out from Jerusalem; half of them toward the former sea, and half of them toward the hinder sea: in summer and in winter shall it be.

9 And **the LORD shall be king over all the earth**: in that day shall there be one LORD, and his name one.

Thus, in reading these verses, especially verse 9, a person would perhaps decide that the final major prophesied event before the actual Second Coming would be this appearance of the Savior to the Jews, followed immediately by His Coming.

However, suppose that during another personal scripture reading session, he or she ends up reading the following verses in Ezekiel and begins to realize that there may still be considerable time between the appearance of the Lord in Jerusalem and His final Coming. Note: These verses deal primarily with the cleanup which will take place after the Lord rescues the Jews from their enemies in the Holy Land in the last days (bold added for emphasis).

Ezekiel 39:8-16.

8 ¶ Behold, it is come, and it is done, saith the Lord GOD; **this *is* the day whereof I have spoken.**

9 And they that dwell in the cities of Israel shall go forth, and shall set on fire and burn the weapons, both the shields and the bucklers, the bows and the arrows, and the handstaves, and the spears, and they shall burn them with fire **seven years**:

10 So that they shall take no wood out of the field, neither cut down *any* out of the forests; for they shall burn the weapons with fire: and they shall spoil those that spoiled them, and rob those that robbed them, saith the Lord GOD.

11 ¶ And it shall come to pass in that day, *that* I will give unto Gog (Israel's enemies who were destroyed by the Lord) a place there of graves in Israel, the valley of the passengers on the east of the sea: and it shall stop the noses of the passengers: and there shall they bury Gog and all his multitude: and they shall call *it* The valley of Hamon-gog.

12 And **seven months** shall the house of Israel be burying of them, that they may cleanse the land.

13 Yea, all the people of the land shall bury *them*; and it shall be to them a renown the day that I shall be glorified, saith the Lord GOD.

14 And they shall sever out men of continual employment, passing through the land to bury with the passengers those that remain upon the face of the earth, to cleanse it: **after the end of seven months** shall they search.

15 And the passengers that pass through the land, **when** *any* **seeth a man's bone, then shall he set up a sign by** it, till the buriers have buried it in the valley of Hamon-gog.

16 And also the name of the city *shall be* Hamonah. Thus shall they cleanse the land.

There are many more examples of such situations which make it difficult and probably impossible for us to calculate with exactness the timing or sequencing of events before the Advent of the Lord. If it were possible to do so, perhaps some would be inclined to calculate how much time they have before the Coming and then live outside the commandments up to a certain time, then begin to become "active" in the Church again, pay tithing etc., supposedly thus getting ready for the arrival of the Savior. We know from Matthew 24:36, as previously quoted in this book, that nobody knows the exact time of His Coming.

WILL THE SAVIOR COME BY THE YEAR 2000?

This may sound like an unnecessary question, since we have now passed up the year 2000. However, there are many who believe, and rightly so, that our calendar is not that accurate. They believe that we have not yet actually arrived at the year 2000, and that when we do, the Savior will come. Many base this belief on the "six seals" in Revelation, chapter six. These six "seals" represent the first 6,000 years of the earth's history after the fall of Adam. These verses from the Book of Revelation are given here, with notes, excerpted from *The New Testament Made Easier, Part 2*, Cedar Fort, Inc., 2003, by David J. Ridges.

1 And I saw when the Lamb (Christ) opened one of the seals (the first one, representing the first thousand years of the earth's temporal existence, i.e., approximately 4000-3000 BC; D&C 77:7), and I heard, as it were the noise of thunder, one of the four beasts saying, Come and see.

2 And I (John) saw, and behold a white horse (symbolically, white can mean righteousness and horse represents victory): and he that sat on him had a bow; and a crown (authority) was given unto him: and he went forth conquering, and to conquer (one possible interpretation could be Adam. Another, Enoch and his victories with the City of Enoch).

3 And when he (Christ) had opened the second seal (3000-2000 BC), I heard the second beast say, Come and see.

4 And there went out another horse that was red (bloodshed, war): and power was given to him (perhaps Satan and wicked worldly leaders during the days of Noah) that sat thereon to take peace from the earth, and that they should kill one another: and there was given unto him a great sword (representing terrible destruction).

5 And when he (Christ) had opened the third seal (2000-1000 BC), I heard the third beast say, Come and see. And I beheld (I looked), and lo a black horse (evil, darkness, despair); and he that sat on him had a pair of balances (representing famine; food had to be carefully measured and meted out) in his hand. (During this seal, Abraham went to Egypt because of famine; Joseph's brothers later came to him in Egypt because of famine; also, the Israelites were held as slaves in Egypt during this period.)

6 And I heard a voice in the midst of the four beasts say,

A measure (two U.S. pints) of wheat for a penny (a day's wages), and three measures of barley for a penny; and see thou hurt not (don't waste) the oil and the wine (ie, terrible famine).

7 And when he (Christ) had opened the fourth seal (1000-0 BC; Assyrian captivity, Ten Tribes are lost about 722 BC; Babylonian captivity about 588 BC; Daniel in lion's den; Romans take over prior to Christ's birth), I heard the voice of the fourth beast say, Come and see.

8 And I looked, and behold a pale horse (not much left of Israel, few righteous people, terrible conditions among the wicked, etc.): and his name that sat on him was Death, and Hell followed with him. And power was given unto them over the fourth part (perhaps meaning not quite as severe destruction as in the wind up scenes of the world in Rev. 9:15) of the earth, to kill with sword (military destruction), and with hunger, and with death (pestilence, plagues), and with the beasts of the earth.

9 And when he (Christ) had opened the fifth seal (0-1000 AD), I saw under the altar (altar represents sacrifice) the souls of them that were slain for the word of God (for the gospel), and for the testimony which they held (i.e., those who gave their lives for the gospel's sake):

10 And they (the people who had given their lives for the gospel) cried with a loud voice, saying, How long, O Lord, holy and true, dost thou not judge and avenge our blood on them (the wicked) that dwell on the earth (i.e., when will the wicked get what's coming to them?; the same question is asked by Joseph Smith in D&C 121 and by Habakkuk in Hab. 1)?

11 And white robes (exaltation; 3:5) were given unto every one of them (the righteous martyrs in vs. 9); and it was said unto them, that they should rest yet for a little season, until their fellowservants also and their

brethren, that should be killed as they were, should be fulfilled (i.e., others would have similar fate throughout earth's remaining history).

12 And I beheld when he (Christ) had opened the sixth seal (about 1000-2000 AD), and, lo, there was a great earthquake; and the sun became black as sackcloth of hair (perhaps black goat hair, used in weaving fabric), and the moon became as blood (i.e., great signs in heaven and earth during this period of time);

13 And the stars of heaven (perhaps including satellites, airplanes etc. in our day) fell unto the earth, even as a fig tree casteth her untimely figs, when she is shaken of a mighty wind.

Note: John now jumps ahead to the Second Coming for a few verses. Caution, do not put the Second Coming in the 6th seal. See headings to Rev. 8 and 9 and D&C 77:13.

14 And the heaven departed (JST "opened") as a scroll when it is rolled together; and every mountain and island were moved out of their places (one continent, one ocean again; D&C 133:22-24, Gen. 10:25).

15 And the kings (wicked political leaders) of the earth, and the great men, and the rich men, and the chief captains, and the mighty men, and every bondman, and every free man (i.e., all the wicked), hid themselves in the dens (caves) and in the rocks of the mountains (like Isaiah said the wicked would do at the Second Coming; see Isaiah 2:19 and 2 Nephi 12, verses 10, 19 and 21);

16 And said to the mountains and rocks, Fall on us, and hide us from the face of him (the Father; Rev. 5:1, 7, 13) that sitteth on the throne, and from the wrath (anger) of the Lamb (Christ):

17 For the great day of his (the Savior's) wrath is come; and who shall be able to stand (i.e., who will be able to

survive the Second Coming)? (Answer: those living a terrestrial or celestial lifestyle. D&C 5:19 plus 76:81–85 and 88:100-101 tell us that those who live the wicked lifestyle of telestials, which includes lying, stealing, sexual immorality, and murder [and of course, sons of perdition] will be destroyed by the Savior's glory at the Second Coming and will not be resurrected until after the Millennium is over.)

As stated above, many interpret these verses in Revelation to mean that the Savior will come at the end of the sixth "seal." They believe this to mean either the beginning of the year 2000 AD or at the end of the year 2000 AD. Because of this mistaken idea, many in recent years have predicted the exact day of the Lord's Coming. They have gathered others around them who abandoned homes and property, resigned their employment etc. and joined together as groups to await the Lord's coming. Needless to say, they have been disappointed.

What such individuals do not understand is that the Savior will not come at the end of the six thousand years. He will come sometime in the beginning of the seventh "seal", in other words, sometime in the beginning of the seventh thousand years. This is clearly stated in the Doctrine and Covenants, where the Lord answered specific questions about the Book of Revelation through the Prophet Joseph Smith. In D&C 77:6, 7, 12 and 13, we read (bold added for emphasis):

> 6 Q. What are we to understand by the book which John saw, which was sealed on the back with **seven seals?**
> A. We are to understand that it contains the revealed will, mysteries, and the works of God; the hidden things of his economy concerning this earth during the **seven thousand years of its continuance**, or its **temporal existence**.
> 7 Q. What are we to understand by the **seven seals** with which it was sealed?

A. We are to understand that **the first seal contains the things of the first thousand years, and the second also of the second thousand years, and so on until the seventh.**

12 Q. What are we to understand by the sounding of the trumpets, mentioned in the 8th chapter of Revelation?
A. We are to understand that as God made the world in six days, and on the seventh day he finished his work, and sanctified it, and also formed man out of the dust of the earth, even so, in the beginning of the seventh thousand years will the Lord God sanctify the earth, and complete the salvation of man, and judge all things, and shall redeem all things, except that which he hath not put into his power, when he shall have sealed all things, unto the end of all things; and the sounding of the trumpets of the seven angels are the preparing and **finishing of his work, in the beginning of the seventh thousand years—the preparing of the way before the time of his coming.**
13 Q. When are the things to be accomplished, which are written in the 9th chapter of Revelation?
A. They are to be **accomplished after the opening of the seventh seal, before the coming of Christ.**

The fact that the Lord will come sometime in the beginning of the seventh thousand year period of the earth's temporal existence certainly eliminates the possibility that anyone could calculate the exact time of His coming!

Just one more note here. We are led by prophets, seers, and revelators in these wonderful last days. As many of you will recall, there was much concern as the world approached the beginning of the year 2000 about how computers would react to the switch to a new century. This great worry was referred to as "Y2K." Amid the hype and concern, which approached panic on some fronts, President James E. Faust, of our First Presidency said the following about Y2K (bold added for emphasis).

> *"Today many people are obsessed with the Y2K problem and worry about the date coming up right because of the way computers measure time. As someone once said about time: '[It] changes with time: in youth, time marches on; in middle age, time flies; and in old age, time runs out.' We have come to rely on electronics for much of our daily work, and we are naturally concerned about the need to reprogram computers to move into the next century.* **While some glitches may occur, I am optimistic that no great catastrophic computer breakdown will disrupt society as we move into the next century.** *I have a far greater fear of the disruption of the traditional values of society."*

When I heard this prophetic statement from President Faust, any concerns which I had previously entertained about Y2K dissolved away to mere curiosity as to what little "glitches," if any, might occur. As you know, there were hardly any at all. What a great blessing to be led by true prophets of God! Confidence and faith in such guidance from them empowers us to follow the Savior's counsel in which He said (bold added for emphasis):

Joseph Smith–Matthew 1:23.

> 23 Behold, I speak these things unto you for the elect's sake; and you also shall hear of wars, and rumors of wars; **see that ye be not troubled**, for all I have told you must come to pass; but the end is not yet.

CHAPTER 3

50 SIGNS OF THE TIMES

As stated earlier in this book, "signs of the times" are prophecies of events and conditions which will indicate that the Second Coming of the Savior is getting close. From the beginning, the Lord has placed these prophecies in the scriptures. Then, by fulfilling them in such open and obvious ways, He provides those who live in the last days with assurance and evidence that He exists and that the scriptures contain the word of God. In addition, any who are honest in heart and some who are not can be drawn toward God by observing the fulfillment of these prophecies.

We will now consider 50 of these signs of the times. We will not intentionally place them in chronological order. We will "treasure them up" in our hearts and use them as they were intended to be used by the Lord, namely, to bear witness to us that the gospel is true, as stated in Joseph Smith–Matthew 1:37-39 (bold added for emphasis):

> 37 And **whoso treasureth up my word, shall not be deceived**, for the Son of Man shall come, and he shall send his angels before him with the great sound of a trumpet, and they shall gather together the remainder of his elect from the four winds, from one end of heaven to the other.
>
> 38 Now learn a parable of the fig-tree—When its branches are yet tender, and it begins to put forth leaves, you know that summer is nigh at hand;
>
> 39 So likewise, **mine elect, when they shall see all these things, they shall know** that he is near, even at the doors;

We will number these prophecies for convenience in refer-ring back to them in this book as well as for the convenience of readers who may be studying them in their own books and then discussing them together. Other than this, **the numbering of these signs of the times in this book has no significance.** As previously noted, there are many more than 50 such signs.

Also, we will divide each of the 50 signs of the times, to be considered in this book, into three general categories as follows:

General Categories:
1. **Already fulfilled**, have already taken place.
2. **Being fulfilled**, that is to say, these signs are currently underway in our day.
3. **Yet future**, in other words, for all intents and purposes, these signs have not yet begun to be fulfilled.

While these are general categories, and obviously there can be some fulfillment of prophecy which may span all three, it is at least interesting to look at each in this way in order to get a feel for the marvelous testimony which is being born to us from the heavens by way of the fulfillment of prophecy in our times.

1. THE DISCOVERY OF AMERICA AND THE ESTABLISHMENT OF THE UNITED STATES OF AMERICA

Category: Fulfilled.

This is a very significant sign of the times. Before the restora-tion could take place, this prophecy had to be fulfilled. The freedoms and environment in which the restoration of the Church could take place had to be established. Nephi prophe-sied the discovery of America by Christopher Columbus and the ensuing colonization by the pilgrims and the colonists as follows:

1 Nephi 13:12-16.

12 And I looked and beheld a man (Columbus) among

the Gentiles, who was separated from the seed of my brethren by the many waters; and I beheld the Spirit of God, that it came down and wrought upon the man; and he went forth upon the many waters, even unto the seed of my brethren (the Lamanites), who were in the promised land.

13 And it came to pass that I beheld the Spirit of God, that it wrought upon other Gentiles (the Pilgrims); and they went forth out of captivity, upon the many waters.

14 And it came to pass that I beheld many multitudes of the Gentiles upon the land of promise; and I beheld the wrath of God, that it was upon the seed of my brethren; and they were scattered before the Gentiles and were smitten.

15 And I beheld the Spirit of the Lord, that it was upon the Gentiles (the colonists), and they did prosper and obtain the land for their inheritance; and I beheld that they were white, and exceedingly fair and beautiful, like unto my people before they were slain.

Nephi continues, prophesying the establishment of the United States of America as follows:

1 Nephi 13:16-19

16 And it came to pass that I, Nephi, beheld that the Gentiles who had gone forth out of captivity did humble themselves before the Lord; and the power of the Lord was with them.

17 And I beheld that their mother Gentiles were gathered together upon the waters, and upon the land also, to battle against them (the 13 Colonies).

18 And I beheld that the power of God was with them, and also that the wrath of God was upon all those that were gathered together against them to battle.

19 And I, Nephi, beheld that the Gentiles that had gone out of captivity were delivered by the power of God out of the hands of all other nations.

1 Nephi 22:7.

> 7 And it meaneth that the time cometh that after all the house of Israel have been scattered and confounded, that the Lord God will raise up a mighty nation among the Gentiles, yea, even upon the face of this land; and by them shall our seed be scattered.

The Savior also prophesied the establishment of the United States as recorded in 3 Nephi 21:4 (bold added for emphasis).

> 4 For it is wisdom in the Father that they should be established in this land, and be **set up as a free people by the power of the Father**, that these things might come forth from them unto a remnant of your seed, that the covenant of the Father may be fulfilled which he hath covenanted with his people, O house of Israel;

By the way, some may suggest that this prophecy is not very current and its fulfillment occurred so far in the past that it should not be considered as a sign of the last days. Actually, in the whole context of the history of the earth since the fall of Adam and Eve, the establishment of the United States of America is very recent. Consider that the earth has seven thousand years from the fall of our first parents to the end of the Millennium and the little season which follows (see D&C 77:6). Thus, the founding of the USA is a relatively recent event in the history of things and is appropriately considered a sign signaling that the Second Coming is getting near.

2. THE COMING FORTH OF THE BOOK OF MORMON

Category: Fulfilled.

The coming forth of the Book of Mormon is a pivotal event in signaling that the last days have arrived. Ezekiel referred to the Bible as "the stick of Judah" and to the Book of Mormon as "the stick of Joseph". In the last days, the Book of Mormon will join with the Bible as a testimony of Christ. This sign of the times is prophesied in Ezekiel 37:15-19 as follows (bold added for emphasis):

> 15 The word of the LORD came again unto me, saying,
> 16 Moreover, thou son of man, take thee one stick, and write upon it, For Judah, and for the children of Israel his companions: then take another stick, and write upon it, For Joseph, the stick of Ephraim, and *for* all the house of Israel his companions:
> 17 And join them one to another into one stick; and they shall become one in thine hand.
> 18 And when the children of thy people shall speak unto thee, saying, Wilt thou not shew us what thou *meanest* by these?
> 19 Say unto them, Thus saith the Lord GOD; Behold, I will take **the stick of Joseph**, which is in the hand of Ephraim, and the tribes of Israel his fellows, and will put them with him, even **with the stick of Judah**, and make them one stick, and they shall be **one in mine hand.**

We mentioned above that the coming forth of the Book of Mormon is a major sign that the last days have begun. This is clearly stated in 3 Nephi 21:1-2, as follows (bold added for emphasis):

> 1 And verily I say unto you, **I give unto you a sign**, that ye may know the time when these things (the gathering and events in the last days as described in 3 Nephi, chapters 20-23) shall be about to take place— that I shall gather in, from their long dispersion, my people, O house of Israel, and shall establish again among them my Zion;
> 2 And behold, **this is the** thing which I will give unto you for a sign—for verily I say unto you **that when**

these things which I declare unto you, and which I shall declare unto you hereafter of myself, and by the power of the Holy Ghost which shall be given unto you of the Father, shall be made known unto the Gentiles (in other words, when the Book of Mormon comes forth) that they may know concerning this people who are a remnant of the house of Jacob, and concerning this my people who shall be scattered by them;

The Savior continues, again explaining that when the record of His dealings with His people in the Americas (the Book of Mormon) comes forth to the remnant of the Lamanites, it is a sign that the last days have begun. In 3 Nephi 21:7, He said (bold added for emphasis):

7 **And when** these things come to pass that **thy seed shall begin to know these things—it shall be a sign unto them**, that they may know that the work of the Father hath already commenced unto the fulfilling of the covenant which he hath made unto the people who are of the house of Israel.

3. THE RESTORATION OF THE PRIESTHOOD AND THE PRIESTHOOD KEYS

Category: Fulfilled.

This is a very important sign of the last days. Without the priesthood, which is the authority of God, delegated to man to act in His name, the Church cannot exist. The Bible informs us that in the last days, before the Coming of the Lord, this priesthood and its attendant powers and keys will be once again available to man on earth. For instance, in Malachi 4:4-6 we read:

5 Behold, I will send you Elijah the prophet before the

coming of the great and dreadful day of the LORD:

6 And he shall turn the heart of the fathers to the children, and the heart of the children to their fathers, lest I come and smite the earth with a curse.

Jeremiah 31:31-33 makes reference to a "new covenant" which will be made in the last days (see heading to Jeremiah 31 in our Bible). Covenants must be made through the power of the priesthood. Therefore, in order for this "new covenant" to be made, the priesthood must be restored. We read:

31 Behold, the days come, saith the LORD, that I will make a new covenant with the house of Israel, and with the house of Judah:

32 Not according to the covenant that I made with their fathers in the day *that* I took them by the hand to bring them out of the land of Egypt; which my covenant they brake, although I was an husband unto them, saith the LORD:

33 But this *shall be* the covenant that I will make with the house of Israel; After those days, saith the LORD, I will put my law in their inward parts, and write it in their hearts; and will be their God, and they shall be my people.

The priesthood and the keys which go with it have been restored as prophesied in the last days. For instance, the Aaronic Priesthood was restored to Joseph Smith and Oliver Cowdery as recorded in D&C 13 as follows:

1. Upon you my fellow servants, in the name of Messiah I confer the Priesthood of Aaron, which holds the keys of the ministering of angels, and of the gospel of repentance, and of baptism by immersion for the remission of sins; and this shall never be taken again from the earth, until the sons of Levi do offer again an offering unto the Lord in righteousness.

The Melchizedek Priesthood was restored by Peter, James and John to Joseph Smith and Oliver Cowdery in the spring of 1829 (see Bible Dictionary, pages 730-731) as mentioned in D&C 27:12-13:

12 And also with Peter, and James, and John, whom I have sent unto you, by whom I have ordained you and confirmed you to be apostles, and especial witnesses of my name, and bear the keys of your ministry and of the same things which I revealed unto them;

13 Unto whom I have committed the keys of my kingdom, and a dispensation of the gospel for the last times; and for the fulness of times, in the which I will gather together in one all things, both which are in heaven, and which are on earth;

Many priesthood keys were restored in the Kirtland Temple on Sunday, April 3, 1836. For instance, Moses and Elias appeared and restored specific keys as recorded in D&C 110:11-12 (bold added for emphasis):

11 After this vision closed, the heavens were again opened unto us; and **Moses appeared** before us, and committed unto us the **keys of the gathering of Israel** from the four parts of the earth, and the leading of the ten tribes from the land of the north.

12 After this, **Elias appeared**, and committed the **dispensation of the gospel of Abraham**, saying that in us and our seed all generations after us should be blessed.

Later in this book, we will deal specifically with the coming of Elijah to restore the keys of the sealing power.

4. THE RESTORATION OF THE TRUE CHURCH OF JESUS CHRIST

Category: Fulfilled.

We are promised in the New Testament and elsewhere that when the last days arrive, the people of the earth will once again have the privilege of joining the true Church of Jesus Christ. Thus, the great apostasy or falling away from the true Church established by the Savior during His mortal ministry will be brought to a close. The Apostle Paul spoke of this apostasy, which would occur before the Savior's return, as follows (bold added for emphasis):

2 Thessalonians 2:1-3.

> 1 Now we beseech you, brethren, by the coming of our Lord Jesus Christ, and *by* our gathering together unto him,
> 2 That ye be not soon shaken in mind, or be troubled, neither by spirit, nor by word, nor by letter as from us, as that **the day of Christ** is at hand.
> 3 Let no man deceive you by any means: for *that day shall not come*, **except there come a falling away first,** and that man of sin be revealed, the son of perdition;

The Apostle, Peter, prophesied the restoration of the true Church of Jesus Christ in the last days before the Second Coming as follows (bold added for emphasis):

Acts 3:19-21.

> 19 Repent ye therefore, and be converted, that your sins may be blotted out, when the times of refreshing shall come from the presence of the Lord;
> 20 And he shall send **Jesus Christ**, which before was preached unto you:

21 **Whom the heaven must receive until the times of restitution of all things**, which God hath spoken by the mouth of all his holy prophets since the world began.

Isaiah prophesied that in the last days the Church would be established in the tops of the mountains and that people throughout the world would come unto it. He said (bold added for emphasis):

Isaiah 2:2-3.

2 And it shall come to pass **in the last days**, *that* the mountain of **the LORD's house shall be established in the top of the mountains**, and shall be exalted above the hills; and **all nations shall flow unto it.**

3 And **many people** shall go and **say**, Come ye, and **let us go up to the mountain of the LORD, to the house of the God of Jacob**; and he will teach us of his ways, and we will walk in his paths:

Surely this prophecy is being fulfilled as people throughout the world look to Salt Lake City, Utah, the headquarters of the true Church of Jesus Christ of Latter-day Saints, established as it were in the tops of the mountains, for guidance from the Lord's living prophets in the last days.

5. THE CHURCH WILL GROW TO FILL THE WHOLE EARTH

Category: Being Fulfilled.

In Daniel, chapter two, we read his exciting prophecy about the spread of the true Church and gospel throughout the whole earth. Daniel explains King Nebuchadnezzar's dream in which the Church was seen as a stone, cut "out of the mountain without hands" which rolled forth and filled the whole earth in the last days. "Without hands" means that it is God's work, not man's. We will quote Daniel 2:35, 44-45 here (bold added for emphasis):

> 35 Then was the iron, the clay, the brass, the silver, and the gold, broken to pieces together, and became like the chaff of the summer threshingfloors; and the wind carried them away, that no place was found for them: and **the stone** that smote the image **became a great mountain, and filled the whole earth**.
>
> 44 And in the days of these kings **shall the God of heaven set up a kingdom, which shall never be destroyed**: and the kingdom shall not be left to other people, *but* it shall break in pieces and consume all these kingdoms, and **it shall stand for ever**.
>
> 45 Forasmuch as thou sawest that the **stone was cut out of the mountain without hands**, and that it brake in pieces the iron, the brass, the clay, the silver, and the gold; the great **God hath made known to the king what shall come to pass hereafter**: and the dream *is* certain, and the interpretation thereof sure.

There are many accounts which bear witness of the fact that this sign of the times is being fulfilled in marvelous ways. Things are happening behind the scenes to prepare for the spread of the gospel throughout the world, including penetrating into countries which now seem off limits to the spread of the gospel.

For example, many years ago, one of my former seminary students told me what had happened to him and his companion as they attempted to teach the gospel in a foreign country whose government was unfriendly to the Church. They had run into so many legal restrictions and government regulations that their work was virtually stopped. In desperation, they decided to go to government headquarters and work their way office by office until they either got to someone who had authority to cut through the legal restrictions so they could do their work, or until they got evicted from the region. Needless to say, they had prayed much about the situation, and this was what they felt prompted to do.

As they entered the government headquarters building, they began to work their plan. As expected, they met bureaucrats in each office who referred them on to the next higher official's office. No one was willing to consider their request for a permit to preach the gospel. This continued for some time until they began to feel that they were wasting their time and the Lord's time. The bureaucracy seemed hopeless. They determined to keep trying for a few more offices since they were now into an area in the building where the offices were quite large and the furnishings rather expensive. Miraculously, no one stopped them. Rather, they simply kept referring them to higher officials. Finally, they found themselves in an extravagantly furnished, spacious office area. The staff members who controlled access to the government official housed there rang his office and were instructed to usher the two young men in.

Upon entering, the missionaries nervously approached the official who was sitting at his large desk and stopped a few feet before reaching the desk. He looked up, put his pen down, stared at them for a few moments, then smiled and said, "You're Americans, aren't you?" in excellent English.

They answered "Yes, sir." He then asked them to tell him where in the United States they were from. My former seminary student told me that, at this point, his main concern was how to explain to the man where Springville, Utah is, as well as the location of his companion's rural Idaho town. Instead, they merely said that they were from the United States and lived east of California. The official smiled and said, "Yes, of course, but be more specific than that. Tell me exactly where you live." My young missionary said, "I live in Springville, Utah, which is about six miles south of Provo, which is about fifty miles south of Salt Lake City." The man quickly came around his desk and vigorously shook their hands saying, "You're Mormon missionaries, aren't you! I know exactly where Springville is. I like Mormons! I went to Brigham Young University in Provo. They treated me very well there. Sit down. What can I do for you?"

A very pleasant conversation followed. Then they explained their problem, and this high government official took immediate action which allowed them to continue the work of the Lord in that area.

Here is yet another example of how the Lord is preparing things for the preaching of the gospel in all the world. Some years ago, the Friday Devotional speaker at the Institute of Religion where I was teaching spoke of some LDS businessmen friends of his who had journeyed to Communist China. They hoped to invest successfully in developing businesses there as trade relations with outside investors opened up. While there, the men were hosted by a government-sponsored young factory worker who spoke excellent English. At the end of their excursion in China, which lasted several weeks, their young host shepherded them to the airport where they awaited their flight home to Utah. A tender friendship had grown between them and the young Chinese interpreter, and as the time of their departure approached, the young man surprised them by presenting them with a wonderful gift.

In their businessmen minds, they quickly calculated that the gift would have cost their host at least one month's wages, and they had nothing to give him in return. Acquiring a gift for him had skipped their minds and they were caught completely off guard. However, one of the businessmen had been reading in his leather-bound triple combination scriptures while awaiting the plane, and a quick-thinking colleague quickly snatched the book from the hands of his friend and presented it to the young Chinese, saying that this book was a gift from them to him, that it contained sacred writings which were most prized by these men, and that it would be an honor to them if he would read it.

The young man caressed the leather cover of the book and the gold-leafed pages, noting the fine quality of the very thin pages of the book, then held the LDS scriptures close to his chest and expressed both gratitude and astonishment that they would give him such a precious treasure. The plane arrived and they parted with deep emotion.

Some months later, the LDS businessmen again flew to China, this time to go ahead with some business deals. Again, the Communist government provided an interpreter and host and to their delight, it was the same young man. As they happily chatted and caught each other up on events which had occurred during their absence, the young man excitedly told them that he had been promoted to be foreman over 5,000 Chinese factory workers. He further reported that they all studied English together at the factory for one hour each day. He asked them "And guess what we read as we study English?" The answer astonished the men and caused great joy in their hearts. "The Book of Mormon!"

The young foreman had made copies of pages from the Book of Mormon out of the Triple Combination the men had given him at the airport. He was using these scriptures to teach English to his workers at the factory. Just think of a future day when missionaries are allowed to preach in that region of the country. Some of these seeds which were planted will have taken root and already be awaiting further nourishment. Thus, in this, and no doubt in countless other ways, the way is being prepared for the going forth of the gospel to "all nations, kindreds, tongues and people." (D&C 42:58.)

One last example of this preparation for the gospel to spread throughout the earth in fulfillment of this great prophecy of Daniel. Some years ago, I was told by an LDS serviceman who served in the Gulf War, that members of the Church were allowed to meet together in Church services by the Arab nations in which they were stationed. This was highly unusual, he told me, because no other Christian religions were allow to do so on Arab soil. When asked the reason for this surprising permission, he simply said that high-ranking Arab government officials had such respect for the Church that they allowed it. One limitation was that members were not allowed to meet in groups of more than 35.

In the October 2001 General Conference of the Church, President Gordon B. Hinckley emphasized the growth of the Church. He said, "We are now a global organization. We have members in more than 150 nations." We have missionaries in unprecedented numbers circling the globe. And with modern electronic satellite technology, the gospel message can be transmitted to members and non-members alike in the farthest flung reaches of the world. Indeed, the prophecy of Daniel is being fulfilled before our very eyes!

6. SLAVES WILL RISE UP AGAINST THEIR MASTERS

Category: Being Fulfilled.

At the end of D&C 87:6, we find a prophecy about "the full end of all nations," meaning that as the Millennium begins and the Savior takes over to rule as "King of kings and Lord of lords" (Revelation 17:14), all other governments will cease to be. We will enjoy a "theocracy" or government by God during the thousand years of peace. D&C 87:6 reads as follows (bold added for emphasis):

> 6 And thus, with the sword and by bloodshed the inhabitants of the earth shall mourn; and with famine, and plague, and earthquake, and the thunder of heaven, and the fierce and vivid lightning also, shall the inhabitants of the earth be made to feel the wrath, and indignation, and chastening hand of an Almighty God, until the consumption decreed hath made **a full end of all nations;**

Leading up to this "full end of all nations" is a significant prophecy which is one of the signs of the times. This prophecy which will be fulfilled as the time of the Second Coming draws close is found in D&C 87:4 (bold added for emphasis):

> 4 And it shall come to pass, after many days, **slaves shall rise up against their masters**, who shall be marshaled and disciplined for war.

As we consider this prophecy, we must be careful not to place it in too narrow of a context in our own minds. Some might have a tendency to restrict its fulfillment to the rising up of the slaves against their masters in the past history of the United States. This would be far too narrow in scope. In this prophecy, the word, "slaves," refers to oppressed people everywhere during the last stages of the world before the Savior's Coming. This would include rebellion against oppressive regimes and cultures. It can include women fighting for equal rights, men fighting for equal opportunity, children leaving family and cultural tradition in order to gain higher education, factions within countries demanding fair representation in their governments, etc. A quote from the Doctrine and Covenants Student Manual, Religion 325, used by our Institutes of Religion, page 195, is helpful here:

"D&C 87:4-5. WHO ARE THE 'SLAVES' WHO SHALL RISE UP AGAINST THEIR MASTERS?"

"This prophecy begins with reference to the Civil War, which was fought over the issue of slavery. Many have therefore assumed that the slaves mentioned in Doctrine and Covenants 87:4 were the blacks who fled north and fought in the Union armies against their former masters. Although that action partially fulfilled the prophecy, Elder Joseph L. Wirthlin suggested a further fulfillment: 'In many cases I am quite sure we all think this has to do particularly with the slaves in the Southern States, but I believe, brethren and sisters, that it was

intended that this referred to slaves all over the world, and I think of those, particularly in the land of Russia and other countries wherein they have been taken over by that great nation and where the people are actually the slaves of those individuals who guide and direct the affairs of Russia and China, and where the rights and the privilege to worship God and to come to a knowledge that Jesus Christ is his Son is denied them' (in Conference Report, Oct. 1958, p. 32)."

And so it is not just by chance that there is so much of political turmoil and "rising up" to shake off the shackles of oppression and unrighteous dominion all around us in our day. It is the fulfillment of prophecy designed to bear witness that every word given by God through His prophets will be fulfilled. It is another reminder to the watchful and faithful that the Coming of the Lord is near.

7. SCATTERED ISRAEL WILL BE GATHERED

Category: Being Fulfilled.

Before the Coming of the Lord, there will be a great gathering of Israel out of all the world. For thousands of years, Israel has been scattered. And who is Israel? Answer: The descendants of Abraham, Isaac and Jacob, plus all those who have joined them in the covenants of the true gospel. Jacob had twelve sons (Genesis, chapters 29 and 30 plus chapter 35, verse 18). Jacob's name was changed to "Israel." Thus, the "Children of Israel" are the "Children of Jacob" and their descendants. They are the descendants of Abraham and Sarah. The Lord made a covenant with Abraham which clearly indicated that his posterity would spread his influence throughout the world. In Abraham 2:9-11 we read (bold added for emphasis):

> 9 And I will make of thee a great nation, and I will bless thee above measure, and make thy name great **among**

all nations, and thou shalt be a blessing unto thy seed after thee, that in their hands **they shall bear this ministry and Priesthood unto all nations**;

10 And I will bless them through thy name; for as many as receive this Gospel shall be called after thy name, and shall be accounted thy seed, and shall rise up and bless thee, as their father;

11 And I will bless them that bless thee, and curse them that curse thee; and in thee (that is, in thy Priesthood) and in thy seed (that is, thy Priesthood), for I give unto thee a promise that this right shall continue in thee, and **in thy seed** after thee (that is to say, the literal seed, or the seed of the body) **shall all the families of the earth be blessed**, even with the blessings of the Gospel, which are the blessings of salvation, even of life eternal.

As mentioned above, Israel has indeed been scattered all over the earth. In about 721 BC (see Bible Dictionary, page 638) Assyria took ten of the tribes of Israel captive and led them away to the north. These have become known as the Lost Ten Tribes. Their return is one of the signs of the times (we will consider that sign next in this book). The Jews were scattered several times throughout history, including the Babylonian captivity about 587 BC.

So, the direction for Israel has been outward throughout the centuries, into all the world. When the gathering of Israel begins in earnest, we know that the last days have arrived. Nephi taught of the scattering and gathering of Israel as follows (bold added for emphasis):

1 Nephi 10:12-14.

12 Yea, even my father spake much concerning the Gentiles, and also concerning the house of Israel, that they should be compared like unto an olive-tree, whose branches should be broken off and should be **scattered**

upon all the face of the earth.

13 Wherefore, he said it must needs be that we should be led with one accord into the land of promise, unto the fulfilling of the word of the Lord, that **we should be scattered upon all the face of the earth.**

14 And **after the house of Israel should be scattered they should be gathered together again**; or, in fine, after the Gentiles had received the fulness of the Gospel, the natural branches of the olive-tree, or the remnants of the house of Israel, should be grafted in, or come to the knowledge of the true Messiah, their Lord and their Redeemer.

Nephi again speaks of the gathering of Israel in the latter days as follows (bold added for emphasis):

1 Nephi 19:16.

16 Yea, then will he remember the isles of the sea; yea, and **all the people who are of the house of Israel, will I gather in**, saith the Lord, according to the words of the prophet Zenos, from the four quarters of the earth.

Isaiah speaks of this last days gathering many times. In this next reference, it appears that Isaiah has seen many forms of our modern transportation system which will be used by converts as they gather to be with the Saints, both in terms of gathering to Zion as well as in gathering to attend General Conference. (Bold added for emphasis.)

Isaiah 5:26-30 (with notes in parentheses from *Isaiah Made Easier*, by David J. Ridges).

26 And he will lift up an ensign (flag, rallying point; the true gospel) to the nations from far, and will hiss (whistle; a signal to gather) unto them from the end of the earth: and, behold, **they shall come with speed swiftly** (modern transportation?):

27 None shall be weary nor stumble among them; none shall slumber nor sleep; neither shall the girdle of their loins be loosed, nor the latchet of their shoes be broken **(they will travel so fast that they won't need to change clothes or even take their shoes off)**:

28 Whose arrows are sharp, and all their bows bent, their horses' hoofs shall be counted like flint, and their wheels like a whirlwind **(trains, airplanes?)**:

29 Their roaring shall be like a lion (airplanes etc?), they shall roar like young lions: yea, they shall roar, and lay hold of the prey **(passengers in modern types of transportation?)**, and shall carry it away safe, and none shall deliver it (the converts, i.e., **none will stop the gathering in the last days)**.

30 And in that day (the Last Days) they shall roar against them like the roaring of the sea: and if one look unto the land, light is darkened in the heavens thereof **(conditions in the last days, war, smoke, pollutions etc.?)**

And how is this final "gathering" to be accomplished? The answer is simple, as explained by the Lord in D&C 39:11 (bold added for emphasis):

11 And if thou do this, I have prepared thee for a greater work. Thou shalt preach the fulness of **my gospel**, which **I have sent forth in these last days**, the covenant which I have sent forth **to recover my people, which are of the house of Israel.**

An article in the July 1998 *Ensign*, by Paul K. Browning, emphasized this aspect of the last days gathering. Quoting from the article, entitled "Gathering Scattered Israel: Then and Now," we read:

"As members of The Church of Jesus Christ of Latter-day Saints, we are taught that these are the last days and that

many of the signs having to do with the Savior's Second Coming are taking place in our lifetime. One of the signs we discuss is found in the 10th article of faith: "We believe in the literal gathering of Israel and in the restoration of the ten tribes." Indeed, the doctrine of the gathering is an important part of our understanding about what is to happen before the Savior's return to earth.

"As Joseph's seed brings others into the Church, these new members are then commissioned likewise to go and spread the gospel. In the aggregate, millions will be gathered to help them in their return to the Lord. But in individual specificity, the Lord told Jeremiah that sometimes the gathering entity will be small: 'I will take you one of a city, and two of a family, and I will bring you to Zion' (Jer. 3:14). Thus, it is only through the work of thousands of missionaries and millions of Church members that those among the nations who want to return actually 'return.' In the beginning decades of the Church, converts were encouraged to relocate to places where the Church was headquartered, whether that was Kirtland, Nauvoo, or Salt Lake City. That particular era has passed. Today those who join the Church are encouraged to gather to its stakes—or to build new stakes. Jacob of the Book of Mormon foresaw this development: 'They shall be gathered home to the lands of their inheritance, and shall be established in all their lands of promise' (2 Ne. 9:2).

"President Harold B. Lee emphasized this understanding of what it means to gather when he said, 'The place of gathering for the Mexican Saints is in Mexico; the place of gathering for the Guatemalan Saints is in Guatemala; the place of gathering for the Brazilian Saints is in Brazil; and so it goes throughout the length and breadth of the whole earth' ("Strengthen the Stakes of Zion," Ensign, July 1973, 5).

"Jacob, Nephi's brother, makes it clear in the allegory of the tame and wild olive trees (see Jacob 5) that the blessings pertaining to the house of Israel belong to all those who are obedient and all who choose to join the gathering.

"In summary, it is clear that ancient prophets foresaw the day of a second gathering. It must have thrilled them to look down the corridors of time and see both the tens of millions of Israel's remnants and many others who would respond to the call to be identified with the covenant of Abraham."

8. THE LOST TEN TRIBES WILL RETURN

Category: Yet Future.

We are going to be rather conservative as we discuss this famous sign of the times. You may wish to nudge it a bit toward the "being fulfilled" category because of the number of converts to the Church in foreign lands as well as some domestically, whose patriarchal blessings indicate that they are from tribes of Israel who are a part of the Lost Ten Tribes. This is fine and is not a problem. However, while there is an obvious gathering of Israel taking place right now, including many from remnants of all of the tribes of Israel scattered throughout the world, the scriptures seem to indicate that a large group known as the Lost Ten Tribes will return before the Second Coming. For this reason, we will consider this sign of the times to be primarily in the "yet future" category. D&C 133:26-33 gives fascinating details about their return as follows:

26 And they who are in the north countries shall come in remembrance before the Lord; and their prophets shall hear his voice, and shall no longer stay themselves; and they shall smite the rocks, and the ice shall flow down at their presence.

27 And an highway shall be cast up in the midst of the great deep.

28 Their enemies shall become a prey unto them,

29 And in the barren deserts there shall come forth pools of living water; and the parched ground shall no longer be a thirsty land.

30 And they shall bring forth their rich treasures unto the children of Ephraim, my servants.

31 And the boundaries of the everlasting hills shall tremble at their presence.

32 And there shall they fall down and be crowned with glory, even in Zion, by the hands of the servants of the Lord, even the children of Ephraim.

33 And they shall be filled with songs of everlasting joy.

Apostle James E. Talmage, in his book, *Articles of Faith*, comments on the return of the Lost Ten Tribes as follows:

*"**Restoration of the Lost Tribes**—From the scriptural passages already considered, it is plain that, while many of those belonging to the Ten Tribes were diffused among the nations, a sufficient number to justify the retention of the original name were led away as a body and are now in existence in some place where the Lord has hidden them. To them the resurrected Christ went to minister after His visit to the Nephites, as before stated. Their return constitutes a very important part of the gathering, characteristic of the dispensation of the fulness of times.*

"To the scriptures already quoted as relating to their return, the following should be added. As a feature of the work of God in the day of restoration we are told: 'And they who are in the north countries shall come in remembrance before the Lord; and their prophets shall hear his voice, and shall no longer stay themselves; and they shall smite the rocks, and the ice shall flow down at their presence. And an highway shall be cast up

in the midst of the great deep. Their enemies shall become a prey unto them, And in the barren deserts there shall come forth pools of living water; and the parched ground shall no longer be a thirsty land. And they shall bring forth their rich treasures unto the children of Ephraim, my servants. And the boundaries of the everlasting hills shall tremble at their presence. And there shall they fall down and be crowned with glory, even in Zion, by the hands of the servants of the Lord, even the children of Ephraim. And they shall be filled with songs of everlasting joy. Behold, this is the blessing of the everlasting God upon the tribes of Israel, and the richer blessing upon the head of Ephraim and his fellows' (D&C 133:26-34.)

"From the express and repeated declaration, that in their exodus from the north the Ten Tribes are to be led to Zion, there to receive honor at the hands of those who are of Ephraim, who necessarily are to have previously gathered there, it is plain that Zion is to be first established." (James E. Talmage, Articles of Faith *[Salt Lake City: Deseret Book Co., 1981], p. 308.)*

Occasionally, members of the Church may hear debates as to whether or not the Ten Tribes are "lost" in the sense that they are scattered throughout the nations of the world and consequently do not know who they are, or whether they are lost as a large group and are hidden somewhere by the Lord. In other words, the debate centers around whether or not they are currently together as a group. There is wisdom in not trying to be a "purist" on this matter, saying "Either they are scattered all over or they are together as a group." It could well be that many of them are scattered abroad in all nations in addition to there being a large group together, whose whereabouts are unknown and whose return will be rather spectacular.

It is significant to note that when Moses appeared in the

Kirtland Temple, as recorded in D&C 110:11, and conferred the keys of gathering upon Joseph Smith and Oliver Cowdery, there seemed to be a differentiation between the "gathering of Israel" and the "leading of the ten tribes from the land of the north." The verse reads as follows (bold added for emphasis):

> 11 After this vision closed, the heavens were again opened unto us; and Moses appeared before us, and **committed unto us the keys** of the **gathering of Israel** from the four parts of the earth, **and** the **leading of the ten tribes from the land of the north**.

This seems to imply that they are two separate undertakings in the last days. From this verse we are also given to understand that our modern prophets hold not only the keys of the gathering of Israel, but also the keys of leading the ten tribes from the north, since these keys were given to Joseph and Oliver by Moses, and since these keys have been handed down continuously to the present day.

9. THE TIMES OF THE GENTILES WILL BE FULFILLED

Category: Being Fulfilled.

Simply put, during the days of the Savior's mortal ministry, the gospel was taken to the Jews. After His resurrection and ascension to heaven, He instructed His Apostles and disciples to take the gospel to the Gentiles also. While there are many definitions of "Gentile," in this case, the word simply means anyone who is not a Jew.

Thus, during the Savior's earthly ministry, the gospel was taken first to the Jews, then to the Gentiles. In the last days, before the Second Coming of Christ, the gospel will be taken first to the Gentiles, then to the Jews. The phrase "times of the Gentiles" appears a number of times in the scriptures in one form or another. We will consider two passages of scripture which contain this exact phrase. Speaking of the Jews, Luke recorded this sign of the times as follows (bold added for emphasis):

Luke 21:24.

> 24 And they shall fall by the edge of the sword, and shall be led away captive into all nations: and Jerusalem shall be trodden down of the Gentiles, **until the times of the Gentiles be fulfilled**.

In D&C 45:25, this same prophecy is given, and the context is that of the last days. In context, it reads as follows (bold added for emphasis):

Doctrine and Covenants 45:22-28.

> 22 Ye say that ye know that **the end of the world cometh**; ye say also that ye know that the heavens and the earth shall pass away;
>
> 23 And in this ye say truly, for so it is; but these things which I have told you shall not pass away until all shall be fulfilled.
>
> 24 And this I have told you concerning **Jerusalem**; and when that day shall come, shall a **remnant** be **scattered among all nations**;
>
> 25 But they shall be gathered again; but they shall remain until the times of the Gentiles be fulfilled.
>
> 26 And in that day shall be heard of wars and rumors of wars, and the whole earth shall be in commotion, and men's hearts shall fail them, and they shall say that Christ delayeth his coming until the end of the earth.
>
> 27 And the love of men shall wax cold, and iniquity shall abound.
>
> 28 And when **the times of the Gentiles** is come in, **a light shall break forth among them that sit in darkness, and it shall be the fulness of my gospel;**

We are living in the day when this prophecy is being

fulfilled. We are living in the "times of the Gentiles." The gospel is being taken to the "Gentiles" through the vast and far-reaching missionary effort of the Church. However, as you have probably observed, we are not yet taking the gospel to the Jews. It is not yet time. While there are some wonderful individual members and converts to the Church who are of the tribe of Judah, the Lord has not yet given the signal to begin concerted efforts at preaching the gospel to the Jews. In fact, as you are perhaps aware, at the time of the publishing of this book, members of the Church who visit the Holy Land are specifically instructed by the Church not to engage in conversations about the Church with citizens of Israel in Israel, nor to answer any of their questions about the gospel. This is because of an agreement between the First Presidency and the government of Israel which was negotiated when the Church determined to build the BYU Jerusalem Center some years ago.

While I was serving as a stake president, one of our missionary couples called me one day from their mission field and with great concern asked me if it was true that they were not allowed to baptize a Jewish couple they had taught who were citizens of Israel. As it turned out, they had met and taught this wonderful couple and they had expressed a desire to be baptized. When the Zone Leader of the mission came to interview the couple for baptism, he discovered that they were citizens of Israel and indicated to them and to the missionaries that they could not be baptized at this time. It would violate the agreement between the Israeli Government and our First Presidency that we would neither proselytize nor baptize any citizens of Israel, until such time as the Israeli government requested and gave permission for us to do so.

The missionaries asked on the phone if such a policy were in place and if so, would I please call the Brethren and confirm that it was still in place. I told them that, as far as I knew, such a policy was still in place, but that I would call Church headquarters in Salt Lake City and confirm it. I did so and was told that it is still in force. I then called the missionaries and explained that it was still the case and that their investigators could rest assured that the time would come when they could join the Church, but that that time had not yet arrived. Also, I suggested that the missionary couple assure their investigators that the Lord would look at their hearts and would accept of their desire to be baptized, so that if they continued to live the principles of the gospel as best they could, and if conditions never changed such that they could receive baptism in this life, they would surely have that opportunity in the spirit world.

While we don't know for sure when the Jews will get the opportunity to receive the gospel on a large scale, many suppose that it will be at the time when the Savior appears to them on the Mount of Olives, just outside of Jerusalem at a time when there is much of destruction in Jerusalem and that region of Israel. We will consider this appearance of the Master, which is also one of the signs of the times, a bit later in this book.

10. THERE WILL BE MUCH OF DESPAIR, DEPRESSION, GLOOM AND DOOM AND EMOTIONAL INSTABILITY

Category: Being Fulfilled.

People seem to be flocking to therapists, counselors, and psychologists in unprecedented numbers. There is much of depression, despair, hopelessness, lack of motivation to do anything, etc. all around us. In Luke 22:26, we find this sign of the time. The phrase "men's hearts failing them" refers to giving up hope, having no more courage, having no faith etc. We will read this verse in context with verses 25 and 27 in order to get the last days setting of this prophecy (bold added for emphasis):

Luke 21:25-27.

> 25 And **there shall be signs** in the sun, and in the moon, and in the stars; and upon the earth distress of nations, with perplexity; the sea and the waves roaring;
> 26 **Men's hearts failing them** for fear, and for looking after those things which are coming on the earth: for the powers of heaven shall be shaken.
> 27 And **then shall they see the Son of man coming** in a cloud with power and great glory.

This same sign of the times is given also in the Doctrine and Covenants as well as in the Pearl of Great Price. They read as follows (bold added for emphasis):

Doctrine and Covenants 45:26.)

> 26 And in that day shall be heard of wars and rumors of wars, and the whole earth shall be in commotion, and **men's hearts shall fail them**, and they shall say that Christ delayeth his coming until the end of the earth.

Doctrine and Covenants 88:91.

> 91 And all things shall be in commotion; and **surely, men's hearts shall fail them**; for fear shall come upon all people.

Moses 7:65-66.

> 65 And it came to pass that Enoch saw the day of the coming of the Son of Man, in the last days, to dwell on the earth in righteousness for the space of a thousand years;
> 66 But **before that day** he saw great tribulations among the wicked; and he also saw the sea, that it was troubled, and **men's hearts failing them**, looking forth with fear for the judgments of the Almighty God, which should come upon the wicked.

Fortunately for the Saints in the last days, there is peace and stability in following the living prophets. We have constant guidance from the Lord through them and through the gift of the Holy Ghost. We, of all people on earth, have the best chance of following the Savior's counsel recorded in Matthew 24:6 as well as in Joseph Smith–Matthew 1:23, wherein He said "see that ye be not troubled." There is peace in righteous doing. We have no need to get caught up in the depression and despair which has become such a common and pervasive problem of our times.

11. THERE WILL BE EXTRAORDINARILY WIDESPREAD SELFISHNESS AND LACK OF CARING FOR OTHERS

Category: Being Fulfilled.

In 2 Timothy 3:2, the Apostle Paul writes to Timothy warning of evils and conditions which will be widespread in the last days (see heading to 2 Timothy, chapter 3, in our Bible.) The conditions warned about include extreme selfishness as given in the following verse (bold added for emphasis):

2 Timothy 3:2.

> 2 For men shall be **lovers of their own selves**, covetous, boasters, proud, blasphemers, disobedient to parents, **unthankful**, unholy,

We see this selfishness and lack of caring for the welfare of others all around us. It is, in fact, a rather prominent sign of the times. It is the opposite of the charity and caring taught by the gospel of Christ. Here again, we are fortunate in our wards and branches to dwell as it were in a society of saints, where love, thoughtfulness, service to one another and deep kindness are a part of our daily living. Indeed, the gospel environment protects us to a great degree from the Satan-sponsored emotional ravages of the last days.

12. THE JEWS WILL RETURN TO JERUSALEM

Category: Fulfilled. Also, Being Fulfilled.

For all practical purposes, this major sign of the times has been fulfilled. Sponsored by Great Britain in the United Nations, the Jews became became a nation in 1948. Thus, the Jews have now returned to the Holy Land and have their own nation and their own government. In the April 1960 General Conference of the Church, Elder George Q. Morris of the Council of the Twelve, said that the Jews have returned. He said (bold added for emphasis):

> *"A third item is God's promise that he would gather Jews to Jerusalem, and I think perhaps we may well now not continue the saying the Jews are going to gather in Jerusalem. **I think now we may well say they have gathered.**" (*Conference Report, April 1960, pp. 100-101.)

Thus, we do not need to wait for this sign of the times to be fulfilled. They are back. However, since the Jews continue to return, virtually daily, some may wish to include the category, "being fulfilled" also as we consider this prophecy.

The Prophet Joseph Smith prophesied the return of the Jews as he spoke to members of the Church in April, 1843. He said (bold added for emphasis):

> *"**Judah must return, Jerusalem must be rebuilt,** and the temple, and water come out from under the temple, and the waters of the Dead Sea be healed. It will take some time to rebuild the walls of the city and the temple, &c.; and **all this must be done before the Son of Man will make His appearance.** There will be wars and rumors of wars, signs in the heavens above and on the earth beneath, the sun turned into darkness and the moon to blood, earthquakes in divers*

places, the seas heaving beyond their bounds; then will appear one grand sign of the Son of Man in heaven. But what will the world do? They will say it is a planet, a comet, &c. But the Son of Man will come as the sign of the coming of the Son of Man, which will be as the light of the morning cometh out of the east." (Joseph Smith, History of The Church of Jesus Christ of Latter-day Saints, 7 vols., *introduction and notes by B. H. Roberts [Salt Lake City: The Church of Jesus Christ of Latter-day Saints, 1932-1951], Vol. 5, page 337.)*

In D&C 133:13, the Jews are instructed to flee to Jerusalem in the last days. This verse reads as follows:

13 And let them who be of Judah flee unto Jerusalem, unto the mountains of the Lord's house.

In yet another passage from the Doctrine and Covenants, we read the following (bold added for emphasis):

Doctrine and Covenants 45:24-25.

24 And this I have told you concerning Jerusalem; and when that day shall come, shall a remnant be scattered among all nations;
25 But **they shall be gathered again**; but they shall remain until the times of the Gentiles be fulfilled.

And so it is that the return of the Jews is a major sign of the times. As we watch this and so many other prophecies being fulfilled, our testimonies should grow and be strengthened. Surely, the Lord is most kind and generous to give us so much obvious evidence that the gospel is true.

13. THE JEWS ACCEPT THE TRUE GOSPEL

Category: Yet Future.

Although there are some faithful Jewish members of the Church already, the fulfillment of this prophecy will not come until large numbers of Jews accept Jesus Christ as the Promised Messiah and join the true Church through baptism and confirmation. Nephi speaks of the time when the Jews will finally believe in Christ as follows:

2 Nephi 30:7.

> 7 And it shall come to pass that the Jews which are scattered also shall begin to believe in Christ; and they shall begin to gather in upon the face of the land; and as many as shall believe in Christ shall also become a delightsome people.

Zechariah spoke of the grace or opportunity to believe in Christ which would be extended to the Jews in the last days when the Savior preserves them from destruction and appears to them. We understand that this will lead to the conversion of large numbers of our Jewish brothers and sisters. Zechariah said (bold added for emphasis):

Zechariah 12:7-10.

> 7 **The LORD also shall save the tents of Judah** first, that the glory of the house of David and the glory of the inhabitants of Jerusalem do not magnify *themselves* against Judah.
>
> 8 **In that day shall the LORD defend the inhabitants of Jerusalem**; and he that is feeble among them at that day shall be as David; and the house of David *shall be* as God, as the angel of the LORD before them.
>
> 9 And it shall come to pass in that day, *that* **I will seek to destroy all the nations that come against Jerusalem.**
>
> 10 And **I will pour upon the** house of David, and upon the **inhabitants of Jerusalem, the spirit of grace** and of supplications: and they shall look upon me whom they have pierced, and they shall mourn for him,

as one mourneth for *his* only *son*, and shall be in bitterness for him, as one that is in bitterness for *his* firstborn.

Zechariah 13:6.

> 6 And *one* shall say unto him, **What *are* these wounds in thine hands**? Then he shall answer, *Those* with which I was wounded *in* the house of my friends.

The Doctrine and Covenants sheds further light upon this scene as follows (bold added for emphasis):

Doctrine and Covenants 45:51-53.

> 51 And then shall the Jews look upon me and say: What are these wounds in thine hands and in thy feet?
> 52 **Then shall they know that I am the Lord**; for I will say unto them: These wounds are the wounds with which I was wounded in the house of my friends. I am he who was lifted up. I am Jesus that was crucified. I am the Son of God.
> 53 And then shall they weep because of their iniquities; then shall they lament because they persecuted their king.

On September 10, 1859, Charles W. Penrose also spoke of this great conversion of the Jews in an article in the *Millennial Star*. He said (bold added for emphasis):

> *"His [Christ's] next appearance will be among the distressed and nearly vanquished sons of Judah. At the crisis of their fate, when the hostile troops of several nations are ravaging the city and all the horrors of war are overwhelming the people of Jerusalem, he will set his feet upon the Mount of Olives, which will cleave and part asunder at his touch. Attended by a host from heaven, he will overthrow and destroy the combined armies of the Gentiles, and appear to the worshipping Jews as the mighty Deliverer and Conquerer so long expected by their*

race; and while love, gratitude, awe, and admiration swell their bosoms, the Deliverer will show them the tokens of his cruci-fixion and disclose himself as Jesus of Nazareth, whom they had reviled and whom their fathers put to death. **Then will unbelief depart from their souls, and the blindness in part which has happened unto Israel be removed.** *" ("The Second Advent," by Charles W. Penrose,* Millennial Star, *Volume 21, September 10, 1859, pp.582-583.)*

14. THE PROPHET ELIJAH WILL COME TO RESTORE THE KEYS OF SEALING

Category: Fulfilled.

This sign of the times was fulfilled on Sunday, April 3, 1836, in the Kirtland Temple, in Kirtland, Ohio, when the Prophet Elijah appeared to the Prophet Joseph Smith and Oliver Cowdery and gave them the keys of sealing families together forever. This monumental event is recorded in D&C 110:13-16 as follows (bold added for emphasis):

13 After this vision had closed, another great and glorious vision burst upon us; for **Elijah** the prophet, who was taken to heaven without tasting death, **stood before us**, and said:

14 Behold, the time has fully come, which was spoken of by the mouth of Malachi—testifying that he [Elijah] should be sent, before the great and dreadful day of the Lord come—

15 To turn the hearts of the fathers to the children, and the children to the fathers, lest the whole earth be smitten with a curse—

16 Therefore, **the keys of this dispensation are committed into your hands; and by this ye may know that the great and dreadful day of the Lord is near, even at the doors.**

It is very interesting to note that faithful Jews celebrate the Passover every year. And as part of their Passover celebration, they have a place setting at the table for Elijah. During the services, they ceremoniously open the door to invite Elijah to come in and take his place of honor at their table, if it so happens that he comes that year. It is a tender and reverent token of their faith that the prophecy about the return of Elijah will be fulfilled. The prophecy is found in Malachi 4:5-6 as follows:

> 5 Behold, I will send you Elijah the prophet before the coming of the great and dreadful day of the LORD:
> 6 And he shall turn the heart of the fathers to the children, and the heart of the children to their fathers, lest I come and smite the earth with a curse.

It is also significant to note that the coming of the Prophet Elijah to Joseph Smith and Oliver Cowdery took place on Easter Sunday. Yes, Sunday, April 3, 1836 (see heading to Doctrine and Covenants, section 110) was Easter Sunday, which means that Jews throughout the world were celebrating Passover when he came.

15. CHRIST WILL COME TO HIS TEMPLE

Category: Fulfilled.

One of the signs of the times is that, in the last days before the Second Coming, there will be an appearance of the Lord in His temple. In Malachi 3:1, we are told specifically that the Lord will come to His temple before the Second Coming. The verse reads as follows (bold added for emphasis):

Malachi 3:1.

> 1 Behold, I will send my messenger, and he shall prepare the way before me: and **the Lord**, whom ye seek, **shall suddenly come to his temple**, even the messenger

of the covenant, whom ye delight in: behold, he shall come, saith the LORD of hosts.

In order for this to take place, there would have to be a temple built. The early Saints built the first temple of this dispensation in Kirtland, Ohio, and the Savior came to it as described in D&C 110:1-10 (bold added for emphasis):

Doctrine and Covenants 110:1-10.

1 The veil was taken from our minds, and the eyes of our understanding were opened.

2 **We saw the Lord standing upon the breastwork of the pulpit**, before us; and under his feet was a paved work of pure gold, in color like amber.

3 His eyes were as a flame of fire; the hair of his head was white like the pure snow; his countenance shone above the brightness of the sun; and his voice was as the sound of the rushing of great waters, even the voice of Jehovah, saying:

4 I am the first and the last; I am he who liveth, I am he who was slain; I am your advocate with the Father.

5 Behold, your sins are forgiven you; you are clean before me; therefore, lift up your heads and rejoice.

6 Let the hearts of your brethren rejoice, and let the hearts of all my people rejoice, who have, with their might, built this house to my name.

7 For behold, **I have accepted this house**, and my name shall be here; and I will manifest myself to my people in mercy in this house.

8 Yea, I will appear unto my servants, and speak unto them with mine own voice, if my people will keep my commandments, and do not pollute this holy house.

9 Yea the hearts of thousands and tens of thousands shall greatly rejoice in consequence of the blessings which shall be poured out, and the endowment with which my servants have been endowed in this house.

10 And **the fame of this house shall spread to foreign lands**; and this is the beginning of the blessing which shall be poured out upon the heads of my people. Even so. Amen.

Obviously, the Savior has also come to other temples built unto Him by the Saints in these latter days. But the basic fulfillment of this particular prophecy occurred in the Kirtland Temple.

16. GENEALOGICAL RESEARCH AND INTEREST IN FAMILY HISTORY WILL SPREAD AS NEVER BEFORE

Category: Being Fulfilled.

This is a most fascinating prophecy to watch as it is being fulfilled. This sign of the times is to be a great surge of interest in seeking information about ones ancestors. It includes the sealing of ancestors together as families, after the keys to do so are restored by Elijah, as discussed with sign number 14 in this book. In Malachi 4:5-6, we read (bold added for emphasis):

5 Behold, I will send you Elijah the prophet before the coming of the great and dreadful day of the LORD:

6 And **he shall turn the heart of the fathers to the children, and the heart of the children to their fathers**, lest I come and smite the earth with a curse.

This prophecy is being fulfilled marvelously and obviously! In 1997, it was reported in *American Demographics* that 64 million Americans had written their own family history or had drawn up a family tree. Additionally, it was stated that some 100 million were at that time involved in searching for their roots. In fact, the only hobbies which were more popular than learning about family history were stamp collecting, gardening and coin collecting. (See *Utah County Journal*, Vol. 28, Issue 3, Sunday, January 12, 1997.)

As you have no doubt observed, this interest in learning about ones ancestors continues to grow. Well over half of the patrons who come to the Church's Family History facility in Salt Lake City are not members of the Church. Yet, the "Spirit of Elijah" is upon them and they are drawn into this marvelous work.

President Boyd K. Packer spoke of the influence of family history work on the living as well as upon the dead as follows:

> *"Family history work has the power to do something for the dead. It has an equal power to do something to the living. Family history work of Church members has a refining, spiritualizing, tempering influence on those who are engaged in it. They understand that they are tying their family together, their living family here with those who have gone before.*
>
> *"Family history work in one sense would justify itself even if one were not successful in clearing names for temple work. The process of searching, the means of going after those names, would be worth all the effort you could invest. The reason: You cannot find names without knowing that they represent people. You begin to find out things about people. When we research our own lines we become interested in more than just names or the number of names going through the temple. Our interest turns our hearts to our fathers—we seek to find them and to know them and to serve them." ("Your Family History: Getting Started," Ensign, August 2003, pp. 12-17.)*

Thus it is that the ongoing fulfillment of this great prophecy, which is a prominent sign of the times, bears specific witness that the gospel is true and that the Savior will come as promised.

17. DANGERS UPON THE WATERS
Category: Being Fulfilled.

This particular sign of the times is much misunderstood and is often the focus of misinformation. It comes from the Doctrine and Covenants, section 61. The problem is that some verses of this revelation are very specific to the time it was given as well as to "these waters" (verse 5, which would be the rivers upon which the saints would travel, including the Missouri River.) Other parts of the revelation can be considered a "sign of the times," such as verses 4, 14 and 15. We will first quote some of the verses from this section, then point out some facts and also some potential problems with interpretation. As usual, we will add bold for teaching purposes plus we will make comments in parentheses in some of the verses..

Doctrine and Covenants 61:4-7.

> 4 Nevertheless, I suffered it that ye might bear record; behold, there are **many dangers upon the waters, and more especially hereafter**; (In the future.)
> 5 For I, the Lord, have decreed in mine anger many destructions upon the waters; yea, and **especially upon these waters**. (The rivers and waters the saints were using to travel to and from Missouri etc.)
> 6 Nevertheless, all flesh is in mine hand, and he that is faithful among you shall not perish by the waters.

Doctrine and Covenants 61:13-19.

> 13 And now, behold, for your good I gave unto you a commandment concerning these things; and I, the Lord, will reason with you as with men in days of old.
> 14 Behold, I, the Lord, in the beginning blessed the waters (see Genesis 1:20-22); but **in the last days, by the mouth of my servant John, I cursed the waters**. (See Revelation 16:3-4.)

15 Wherefore, **the days will come that no flesh shall be safe upon the waters**. (Future prophecy, a sign of the times. Perhaps including pollution, toxic waste, oil spills, giardia, etc.)

16 And it shall be said in days to come that none is able to go up to the land of Zion upon the waters, but he that is upright in heart. (Specific reference to travel to Missouri in that day.)

17 And, as I, the Lord, in the beginning cursed the land (Genesis 3:17), even so in the last days have I blessed it (D&C 104:14-18), in its time, for the use of my saints, that they may partake the fatness thereof. (A prophecy that agricultural science will greatly increase productivity of the land in the last days.)

18 And now I give unto you a commandment that what I say unto one I say unto all, that you shall **forewarn your brethren concerning these waters**, that they come not in journeying upon them, lest their faith fail and they are caught in snares; (A specific reference to traveling on those rivers in flood season back then.)

19 I, the Lord, have decreed, and **the destroyer rideth upon the face thereof**, and I revoke not the decree. (Satan will wield power and cause troubles with water in the last days.)

Doctrine and Covenants 61:22.

22 And **it mattereth not unto me**, after a little, if it so be that they fill their mission, **whether they go by water or by land**; let this be as it is made known unto them according to their judgments hereafter (in other words, use common sense). (It is ok for Latter-day Saints to travel in water craft, as long as they use common sense.)

In conclusion, it is obvious that one of the signs of the times is that there will be extra dangers upon the waters and because of the waters, in the last days. This can include more frequent, more violent storms, oil spills, toxins being poured into rivers and streams, acid rain, warships, torpedoes, the spread of destructive algae, etc. We will deal more with some of this in the next sign we consider. However, there is much misinformation and even LDS "mythology" which has grown up around this issue. For instance, missionaries are not allowed to go swimming during their missions. Some members attribute this to the notion that some evil force awaits to pull them under and drown them. Yet, in some missions, including Elder John H. Groberg's mission to the South Pacific, traveling by boat, ship, canoe, or whatever is almost a daily necessity. Perhaps one of the real reasons that missionaries are not allowed to go swimming is that the scenery at the beach or in the swimming pool is too immodest. In other words, very little fabric is used for a large number of swimming suits, which can make it difficult if not impossible for missionaries to avoid lustful thoughts. Lustful thinking drives the Spirit away. (See D&C 42:23.)

18. MUCH ECOLOGICAL DAMAGE WILL OCCUR IN THE LAST DAYS

Category: Being Fulfilled.

The Book of Revelation seems to especially point out this sign of the times, particularly in chapter 8. We will put these verses here and then bold some words and phrases so that you can see at-a-glance what we mean.

Revelation 8:7-12.

> 7 The first angel sounded, and there followed hail and fire mingled with blood, and they were cast upon the earth: and the third part of **trees** was burnt up, and all green grass was burnt up.

8 And the second angel sounded, and as it were a great mountain burning with fire was cast into the sea: and the third part of the **sea** became blood;

9 And the third part of the creatures which were in the **sea,** and had life, died; and the third part of the **ships** were destroyed.

10 And the third angel sounded, and there fell a great star from heaven, burning as it were a lamp, and it fell upon the third part of the **rivers,** and upon the **fountains of waters;**

11 And the name of the star is called Wormwood: and the third part of the **waters** became wormwood; and many men died of the **water**s, because they were **made bitter.**

12 And the fourth angel sounded, and the third part of the **sun** was smitten, and the third part of the **moon,** and the third part of the **stars**; so as the third part of them was darkened, and the day shone not for a third part of it, and the night likewise.

There are obviously many ways in which the damage to the environment, indicated in the foregoing verses could be inflicted. In conclusion, it would appear from these and other verses in scripture that there will be prominent ecological damage and disturbance in the last days leading up to the Coming of the Lord.

19. THE SUN WILL BE DARKENED AND THE MOON WILL BECOME AS BLOOD

Category: Fulfilled

For many years, as I spoke on the signs of the times at Know Your Religion lectures, Education Week, forums and in classes, I suggested to my students that we would be wise not to define nor to categorize this particular sign of the times. My reason for such thinking was that I had never heard a prophet even explain this prophecy, let alone say whether or not it had happened or was yet to be fulfilled. Then, in October General Conference of 2001, in the Saturday morning session, President Gordon B. Hinckley said something that changed my mind on this prophecy. He said (bold added for emphasis):

> *"The era in which we live is the fulness of times spoken of in the scriptures, when God has brought together all of the elements of previous dispensations. From the day that He and His Beloved Son manifested themselves to the boy Joseph, there has been a tremendous cascade of enlightenment poured out upon the world. The hearts of men have turned to their fathers in fulfillment of the words of Malachi. **The vision of Joel has been fulfilled wherein he declared:**

Joel 2:28-32.

> 28 And it shall come to pass afterward, *that* I will pour out my spirit upon all flesh; and your sons and your daughters shall prophesy, your old men shall dream dreams, your young men shall see visions:
>
> 29 And also upon the servants and upon the handmaids in those days will I pour out my spirit.
>
> 30 And I will shew wonders in the heavens and in the earth, blood, and fire, and pillars of smoke.
>
> 31 **The sun shall be turned into darkness, and the moon into blood, before the great and the terrible day of the LORD come.**
>
> 32 And it shall come to pass, *that* whosoever shall call on the name of the LORD shall be delivered: for in mount Zion and in Jerusalem shall be deliverance, as the LORD hath said, and in the remnant whom the LORD shall call."

As soon as our living Prophet said that these words of Joel have been fulfilled, I accepted it on faith. We are now left to wonder how these prophetic words have been fulfilled, and until if and when the Prophet explains further, we will have to wait for further understanding. There are other prominent references to the sun's being darkened and the moon's being turned to blood. For instance (bold added for emphasis):

Matthew 24:29.

> 29 Immediately after the tribulation of those days shall the **sun** be **darkened**, and the **moon shall not give her light**, and the stars shall fall from heaven, and the powers of the heavens shall be shaken:

Revelation 6:12.

> 12 And I beheld when he had opened the sixth seal, and, lo, there was a great earthquake; and **the sun became black as sackcloth** of hair, and **the moon became as blood**;

As mentioned above, we will have to wait for a prophet to reveal the exact meaning of these words to us. In the meantime, many people have felt that this prophecy has to do with air pollution. However, there have no doubt been events in centuries past such as earthquakes, volcanos and the like which would have caused great air pollution and thus darkened the sun and made the moon to appear as blood. Thus, air pollution is probably not a very good possibility for the fulfillment of this prophecy.

Perhaps we need to rethink, after President Hinckley's words on this subject, and begin to wonder if the meaning could be more symbolical than literal. For instance, in our gospel vocabulary, we often use the sun to symbolize celestial glory, heaven, light from above, etc. The moon often symbolizes terrestrial glory, which implies good and honorable people (see D&C 76:75), keeping the law of chastity, moral integrity, etc. One possibility, though certainly not authoritative, could be that the sun's being darkened and the moon's becoming as blood would symbolize gross spiritual darkness in the final days preceding the Second Coming. It may symbolize that the vast majority of the inhabitants of the earth will cease to live according to either celestial or terrestrial law. It could mean that throughout the world, there will be an overflowing flood of indulging in filth and spiritual pollution, adultery, fornication, homosexuality, lesbianism, pornography, dishonesty, crudeness, selfishness, etc., etc. The list goes on and on as described in D&C 76:103, Revelation 15:22 and elsewhere. Whatever the case, we will consider this sign of the time fulfilled, based on President Hinckley's statement, and we will look forward to additional authoritative instruction on the matter.

20. DISEASES, PLAGUES, AND PESTILENCES WILL SWEEP THE EARTH IN SPITE OF MEDICAL ADVANCES AND TECHNOLOGY

Category: Being Fulfilled.

Advances in medical science are, for the most part, wonderful and serve as a great blessing from God to His children here on earth. Many of us owe our lives or the quality of life we enjoy to medical advances which have been achieved in our day. We owe a great debt of gratitude to the tireless efforts and great skill of medical practitioners who have dedicated their lives to curing disease and taking care of their patients.

However, in spite of all the advances in medical science, this sign of the times prophesies that great plagues, diseases, pestilences etc. will sweep the earth. God will not be mocked. The Prophet Joseph Smith spoke of the wicked throughout the world and warned what would happen if they reject the gospel and fight against truth. In D&C 109:30 he said (bold added for emphasis):

30 And that all their works may be brought to naught,

and **be swept away by the hail, and by the judgments which thou wilt send upon them in thine
anger**, that there may be an end to lyings and slanders
against thy people.

2 Nephi 6:14-15 says (bold added for emphasis):

14 And behold, according to the words of the prophet,
**the Messiah will set himself again the second
time to recover them** (the restoration in the latter
days); wherefore, he will manifest himself unto them in
power and great glory, unto the destruction of their
enemies, when that day cometh when they shall believe
in him; and none will he destroy that believe in him.

15 And **they that believe not in him shall be
destroyed**, both by **fire**, and by **tempest**, and by
earthquakes, and by **bloodsheds**, and by **pestilence**,
and by **famine**. And they shall know that the Lord is
God, the Holy One of Israel.

D&C 84:97 tells us (bold added for emphasis):

97 And **plagues shall go forth,** and they shall not be
taken from the earth until I have completed my work,
which shall be cut short in righteousness—

D&C 87:6 adds (bold added for emphasis):

6 And thus, **with** the **sword** and by **bloodshed** the
inhabitants of the earth shall mourn; and with **famine**,
and **plague**, and **earthquake,** and the **thunder** of
heaven, and the fierce and vivid **lightning** also, **shall
the inhabitants of the earth be made to feel the
wrath, and indignation, and chastening hand of
an Almighty God**, until the consumption decreed
hath made a full end of all nations;

Joseph Smith–Matthew 1:29 repeats this prophecy of the last

days as follows (bold added for emphasis):

> 29 Behold I speak for mine elect's sake; for nation shall rise against nation, and kingdom against kingdom; there shall be famines, and **pestilences,** and earthquakes, in divers places.

In conclusion, it is clear from these scriptural passages and others that God will not be mocked by people who seemingly get away with blatant sin because of medical advances. Rather, He will send plagues, pestilences, diseases, etc. to sweep the earth in an effort to get people to use their agency to repent and return to Him. We will finish our consideration of this sign of the times with D&C 45:31 (bold added for emphasis):

> 31 And there shall be men standing in that generation, that shall not pass until they shall see **an overflowing scourge**; for **a desolating sickness shall cover the land**.

By the way, the phrase "desolating sickness" in verse 31, above, doesn't necessarily have to be limited to just one form of disease or plague. In fact, it may also include spiritual darkness, which is the worst form of disease.

21. KNOWLEDGE, SCIENCE, AND TECHNOLOGY WILL INCREASE DRAMATICALLY

Category: Being Fulfilled.

This is a fascinating sign of the last days. We indeed live in a day of unprecedented advances in all forms of knowledge and technology. President Hinckley spoke of this during the Saturday morning session of the 2001 General Conference of the Church. He said:

"There has been more of scientific discovery during these years than during all of the previous history of mankind. Transportation, communi-

cation, medicine, public hygiene, the unlocking of the atom, the miracle of the computer, with all of its ramifications, have blossomed forth, particularly in our own era. During my own lifetime, I have witnessed miracle after wondrous miracle come to pass."

Daniel recorded this prophecy of a latter-day increase in knowledge in Daniel 12:4 when he wrote the word of the Lord as follows (bold added for emphasis):

> 4 But thou, O Daniel, shut up the words, and seal the book, *even* to **the time of the end**: many shall run to and fro, and **knowledge shall be increased.**

It even sounds like the phrase "many shall run to and fro" could refer to modern transportation and the resulting hustle and bustle of society in the last days.

It is interesting to pay attention to the timing when so many of these advances have come onto the scene. If you were to take a large chalkboard and begin to plot inventions from about 4,000 BC and continue to the present day, putting one dot on the board for each invention which advanced the status of mankind, you would find very few dots until about the time of the restoration of the gospel through Joseph Smith. Then, the frequency of advances in all sorts of endeavor would begin to increase dramatically. Just a few examples follow:

> 1840s–The discovery of germs by Dr. Semmelweis, Vienna, Austria.
>
> 1846–The first large-scale demonstration of general anesthesia, Massachusetts General Hospital, Boston.
>
> 1868–The typewriter.
>
> 1869–The telegraph.
>
> 1876–The telephone.
>
> 1877–The phonograph.
>
> 1877–Arc welding.
>
> 1879–The light bulb.
>
> 1880s–The Kodak camera.

1880–The pneumatic tire.

1884–The fountain pen.

1888–The ball point pen.

1890s–The automobile.

1890s–Silent movies.

1890s–Marconi's radio crystal.

1891–Forerunner of the zipper.

1893–Half-tone printing.

1898–Photographic paper.

1899–Magnetic tape recorder.

1903–Wright Brother's airplane.

1907–Radio tube.

1915–Tungsten filament for light bulbs etc.

1920–Talking movies.

1934–Television.

1937–Jet engine.

1939–Computer.

1947–Transistor.

And if we were to attempt to continue the list from 1947 up to the current day, it would be a virtually impossible task. In D&C 88:73, the Lord said "I will hasten my work in its time." Indeed, He has inspired the means and technology to hasten the spread of the gospel throughout the world. If you look at the brief and limited list of inventions given above, you will note that many of the inventions have to do with communication and transportation. Certainly, this is part of the grand plan of the Lord to enable the true gospel to be preached to all the world before the end comes.

22. WARS AND RUMORS OF WARS WILL BECOME NORMAL LIFE

Category: Being Fulfilled.

This prophecy seems to indicate that wars and rumors of impending wars will become so commonplace that people will hardly pay any attention to them in the news. They will go about their daily lives and only particularly notice especially spectacular war news or those incidents which directly affect them. This is a much prophesied sign of the times. We will give just a few of the many scripture references to this sign (bold added for emphasis)

Matthew 24:6.

> 6 And ye shall hear of **wars and rumours of wars**: see that ye be not troubled: for all *these things* must come to pass, but the end is not yet.

Joseph Smith–Matthew:23.

> 23 Behold, I speak these things unto you for the elect's sake; and you also shall hear of **wars, and rumors of wars**; see that ye be not troubled, for all I have told you must come to pass; but the end is not yet.

Doctrine and Covenants 45:26.

> 26 And in that day shall be heard of **wars and rumors of wars**, and the whole earth shall be in commotion, and men's hearts shall fail them, and they shall say that Christ delayeth his coming until the end of the earth.

Several years ago, I read in the newspaper that there were 53 declared wars going on at that time in various places throughout the world, plus many undeclared wars. I don't know how many there are today, but suspect that there are many more than that. Perhaps one of our challenges as children of God living in such conditions in the last days is to avoid becoming callous to human suffering around us.

23. FAMINES, EARTHQUAKES, TORNA-DOES, AND NATURAL DISASTERS WILL ABOUND

Category: Being Fulfilled.

This sign of the times is being fulfilled around the globe in very obvious and observable ways. It, too, is mentioned in several scriptural references. For instance, D&C 45 (bold added for emphasis):

Doctrine and Covenants 45:33.

> 33 And there shall be **earthquakes** also in divers places, and **many desolations**; yet men will harden their hearts against me, and they will take up the sword, one against another, and they will kill one another.

It is interesting to note that the Lord explains His reasoning for sending these increased natural disasters upon the earth. In fact, He explains that these things follow on the heels of gentler approaches to bring His wayward children back to the blessings of the gospel. And when the inhabitants of the earth ignore these gentler approaches, the calm and fervent testimonies of members and missionaries sent throughout the earth to proclaim the message of peace and salvation through the gospel of Jesus Christ, then He uses more spectacular ways to get their attention, that they might repent and come unto Him through Christ. One passage of scripture which explains it this way is D&C 88:88-91 (bold added for emphasis):

> 88 And **after your testimony** cometh wrath and indignation upon the people.
> 89 For **after your testimony** cometh the **testimony of earthquakes,** that shall cause groanings in the midst of her, and men shall fall upon the ground and shall not be able to stand.
> 90 And also cometh the **testimony of the voice of**

thunderings, and the voice of **lightnings**, and the voice of **tempests**, and the voice of the **waves of the sea heaving themselves beyond their bounds.**

91 And **all things shall be in commotion**; and surely, men's hearts shall fail them; for fear shall come upon all people.

Occasionally, people are heard to suggest that there is actually not an increase in these natural disasters. Rather, it is just that we have more sensitive and better scientific instruments with which to measure and record these events. Some years ago, an acquaintance of mine wrote to a local meteorologist and asked him if this might be the case. His reply was definite. He said that there is definitely an increase both in frequency and intensity of these natural disasters. Something is going on. Since that time, I have seen numerous articles in newspapers and magazines supporting the fact that nature seems to be more and more in commotion. This sign of the times is being fulfilled.

24. STRIKES, OVERTHROWING OF GOVERNMENTS, GANG WARFARE, VIOLENCE, AND DISRESPECT FOR AUTHORITY WILL INCREASE

Category: Being Fulfilled.

Elder Bruce R. McConkie summarized this sign of the last days as follows:

"STRIKES, ANARCHY, VIOLENCE, TO INCREASE. — Not only do disasters and perils abound because of the unsettled conditions of the elements, but that same spirit of unrest is found among men themselves. The Lord's decree for this age is: 'The whole earth shall be in commotion.' (D. & C. 45:26.) Signs of this commotion are seen daily in the untempered strikes and labor troubles that rock the economic world; in the violence, compulsion, and

destruction of property that attend these strikes; in the unholy plots against our freedoms and free institutions; in the anarchy, rebellion, and crime that flow from great political movements which seek to destroy the agency of man and overthrow the governments of the world by force and violence. Communism and every other brutal and evil association or form of govern- ment are signs of the times." (Bruce R. McConkie, Mormon Doctrine, *2d ed. [Salt Lake City: Bookcraft, 1966], 726.)*

Isaiah spoke of the disrespect for authority, for parents, and the resulting anarchy (lack of effective leadership in communi- ties, nations etc.), which would lead to the downfall of Jerusalem in ancient times. Satan will cause the same attitudes and trends to abound in the days directly preceding the Second Coming. Isaiah warned (bold added for emphasis):

Isaiah 3:5.

5 And the **people shall be oppressed, every one by another,** and **every one by his neighbour**: the **child shall behave himself proudly against the ancient,** and **the base against the honourable.**

The Apostle Paul warned of these same conditions and prophesied that they would exist on a broad scale in the last days. He said (bold added for emphasis):

2 Timothy 3:1-4.

1 This know also, that **in the last days perilous times shall come.**

2 For men shall be lovers of their own selves, covetous, boasters, proud, blasphemers, **disobedient to parents,** unthankful, unholy,

3 Without natural affection, **trucebreakers,** false accusers, incontinent, fierce, **despisers of those that are good,**

4 **Traitors,** heady, highminded, lovers of pleasures more than lovers of God;

In the book of Helaman, in the Book of Mormon, we find a very straightforward description of how governments, which were set up based on correct principles, can become corrupt which leads to unreasonable strikes, anarchy, disrespect for good and honorable principles and people, and ultimately the destruction of society. Simply put, the steps are as follows:

1. The original government is set up, based on the commandments of God.
2. Moral, righteous citizens endorse and support the government.
3. Over time, citizens become wicked and can't stand righteous laws.
4. The laws of the land are changed to support corrupt lifestyles of citizens.
5. People begin to use corrupt laws to support personal wickedness. They no longer ask, "What does the Bible say?" Rather, they ask, "Is it legal?"
6. Thus, corrupt laws corrupt people and corrupt people continually pass additional corrupt laws until society becomes morally bankrupt.
7. People are no longer governed in their own hearts by personal righteousness. Therefore, anarchy, violence, etc. result in the destruction of society.

This cycle of apostasy is described in Helaman 4:21-23 as follows (bold added for emphasis):

21 Yea, they began to remember the prophecies of Alma, and also the words of Mosiah; and they saw that **they had been a stiffnecked people**, and that **they had set at naught the commandments of God**;
22 And that **they had altered and trampled under their feet the laws of Mosiah**, or that which the Lord commanded him to give unto the people; and they saw that **their laws had become corrupted**,

and that **they had become a wicked people**, insomuch that they were wicked even like unto the
Lamanites.

23 And **because of their iniquity** the church had
begun to dwindle; and they began to disbelieve in the
spirit of prophecy and in the spirit of revelation; and
the judgments of God did stare them in the face.

As we watch this sign of the times being fulfilled, we would
do well to follow the counsel of the Brethren who repeatedly
have requested that we become involved in our own community
and government entities in order to exert influence to stem the
tide of corruption which is leading to the fulfilling of this
prophecy.

25. SEXUAL IMMORALITY, HOMOSEXUALITY, LESBIANISM, AND PORNOGRAPHY WILL ABOUND

Category: Being Fulfilled.

Many would wish that we could categorize this sign of the
times as "fulfilled." However, since it will continue to get worse
until the Savior comes, we must leave it as "being fulfilled."
There are many warnings in the scriptures that this will be the
case in the last days. It seems that the prophecy implies that
sexual immorality will become so widespread and common in
the last days that it will be considered to be the norm, and that
anyone who does not get involved with these pernicious evils
will be considered to be strange or abnormal.

The Apostle Paul speaks of this widespread last days evil in
his letter to Timothy. We will use 2 Timothy 3:1 and 6 (bold
added for emphasis):

1 This know also, that **in the last days perilous times
shall come**.

6 For of this sort are they which creep into houses, and
lead captive silly women laden with sins, **led away
with divers lusts,**

Paul speaks of "diverse lusts" in prophesying about the last
days. It is important for us to understand what he meant by this
term. By the time he wrote this letter to Timothy, he had already
defined a number of "various" lusts, including various types of
sexual immorality, in more detail in his letter to the Romans. As
we quote these verses from Romans, we will include some definitions of terms used by Paul taken from *Strong's Exhaustive
Concordance of the Bible* (in parentheses). Paul warned the Roman
saints as follows (bold added for emphasis):

Romans 1:24-31.

24 Wherefore God also gave them up to uncleanness
through the **lusts of their own hearts,** to **dishonour
their own bodies between themselves** (masturba-
tion):

25 Who changed the truth of God into a lie, and
worshipped and served the creature more than the
Creator, who is blessed for ever. Amen.

26 For this cause God gave them up unto **vile affec-
tions:** for even **their women did change the
natural use into that which is against nature**
(lesbianism):

27 And likewise also the **men, leaving the natural use
of the woman, burned in their lust one toward
another; men with men working that which is
unseemly** (homosexuality), and receiving in themselves that recompence of their error which was meet.

28 And even as they did not like to retain God in *their*
knowledge, God gave them over to a reprobate mind,
to do those things which are not convenient (things
which are not proper);

29 Being filled with all unrighteousness, **fornication,**

wickedness, covetousness, maliciousness; full of envy, murder, debate, deceit, malignity; whisperers,

30 Backbiters, haters of God, despiteful, proud, boasters, inventors of evil things, disobedient to parents,

31 Without understanding, covenantbreakers, **without natural affection**, implacable, unmerciful:

In "The Family: A Proclamation to the World, September 23, 1995, our First Presidency and Quorum of the Twelve Apostles included breaking of the law of chastity in the evils which would bring upon the world the last days calamities spoken of in scripture. They said (bold added for emphasis):

> *"We warn that **individuals who violate covenants of chastity**, who abuse spouse or offspring, or who fail to fulfill family responsibilities **will one day stand accountable before God**. Further, **we warn that the disintegration of the family will bring upon individuals, communities, and nations the calamities foretold by ancient and modern prophets.**"*

In spite of the warnings of our modern prophets, we watch as our society and the world in general become increasingly entangled in the evil web of pornography, sexual immorality, homosexuality, lesbianism, and a host of other evils associated with uncontrolled carnality, lust, and greed. We are no doubt seeing part of the fulfillment of the prophecy found in 2 Nephi 27:1-2. Nephi says that in the last days, people will be "drunken with iniquity," in other words, out of control with wickedness. Surely, the huge emphasis on sexual immorality in our day is part of this sign of the times. We read (bold added for emphasis):

1 But, behold, **in the last days**, or in the days of the Gentiles—yea, behold all the nations of the Gentiles and also the Jews, both those who shall come upon this land and those who shall be upon other lands, yea, even

upon all the lands of the earth, behold, **they will be drunken with iniquity and all manner of abominations—**

2 And when that day shall come they shall be visited of the Lord of Hosts, with thunder and with earthquake, and with a great noise, and with storm, and with tempest, and with the flame of devouring fire.

In conclusion, we read in the Doctrine and Covenants, section 42, that sexual immorality, unrepented of, leads to the loss of the Spirit. When people lose the help of the Spirit, they become easy targets for the devil and his evil hosts. They lose their ability to reason clearly and to even see the dangers of sin. D&C 42:23 reads as follows (bold added for emphasis):

23 And he that looketh upon a woman **to lust** after her shall deny the faith, and **shall not have the Spirit**; and if he repents not he shall be cast out.

One of the ways Satan is weakening people's resistance to the wiles of sexual immorality in our day is through the use of "politically correct" vocabulary to describe it. Such politically correct terminology tends to take away any implication of wrong doing or sin associated with immoral behavior. In the April, 1996, General Conference of the Church, Elder Neal A. Maxwell of the Quorum of the Twelve counseled members about such politically correct terminology. He said (bold added for emphasis):

*"The more what is **politically correct** seeks to replace what God has declared correct, the more ineffective approaches to human problems there will be, all reminding us of C. S. Lewis's metaphor about those who run around with fire extinguishers in times of flood. For instance, there are increasing numbers of victims of violence and crime, yet special attention is paid to the rights of criminals. Accompanying an ever*

increasing addiction to pornography are loud alarms against censorship. Rising illegitimacy destroys families and threatens the funding capacities of governments; nevertheless, **chastity and fidelity are mocked.** *These and other consequences produce a harsh cacophony. When Nero fiddled as Rome burned, at least he made a little music!* **I have no hesitancy, brothers and sisters, in stating that unless checked, permissiveness, by the end of its journey, will cause humanity to stare in mute disbelief at its awful consequences.**

"Ironically, as some people become harder, they use softer words to describe dark deeds. *This, too, is part of being sedated by secularism! Needless abortion, for instance, is a* **"reproductive health procedure,"** *which is an even more "spongy expression" than* **"termination of pregnancy"** *(George McKenna, "On Abortion: A Lincolnian Position," Atlantic Monthly, Sept. 1995, 52, 54). "Illegitimacy" gives way to the wholly sanitized words* **"nonmarital birth"** *or* **"alternative parenting"** *(Ben J. Wattenberg, Values Matter Most [1995], 173). Church members will live in this wheat-and-tares situation until the Millennium." (Neal A. Maxwell, "Becometh As a Child," Ensign, May 1996, page 68.)*

Several years ago, I began collecting "politically correct" terms used by the media and often required by government entities to describe what the word of the Lord calls sin and wickedness. A partial list follows:

Pro-choice: Implies agency is preserved in choosing abortion on demand, thus making an evil choice appear ok. Those who oppose this evil appear somehow anti-choice and thus, anti-God.

Free love: Again, an evil play on words, trying to eliminate the concept of consequences.

Consenting adults: Implies an "ok-ness" if adults do it, even though it is a sin next to murder in seriousness (Alma 39:5.)

Significant others: A sneaky description of one with whom adultery or fornication is committed.

Alternate lifestyles: Makes homosexuality, lesbianism, etc. look like harmless use of agency.

Sexual preference: Treats homosexuality, etc., as a simple matter of personal preference, not sin.

Safe sex: As if illicit sex had no spiritual or emotional penalties at all.

Sexually active: Rather than calling them adulterers and fornicators, etc., thus attempting to remove any hint of wrong-doing or breaking God's commandments.

26. THE SPIRIT WILL STOP WORKING WITH THE WICKED

Category: Being Fulfilled.

When the Spirit stops working with the wicked, they lose their ability to understand the need for personal righteousness. Righteous people are seen as their enemies, and a threat to personal freedom and independence, a threat to the exercising of their agency. Without the Spirit, one's conscience has less and less influence, and evil deeds and cruelty become routine. In D&C 63:32, the Lord tells us that already, in 1831, He was holding His spirit back because of widespread wickedness. He said (bold added for emphasis):

32 I, the Lord, am angry with the wicked; **I am holding my Spirit from the inhabitants of the earth.**

As we read this verse, though, we must be careful to keep it in the larger context of all the scriptures. If we keep it in that larger context, we will see that His Spirit is indeed working with many people everywhere whose deeds and lifestyles have not put them beyond reach of its influence. In D&C 95:4, we read (bold added for emphasis):

> 4 For the preparation wherewith I design to prepare mine apostles to prune my vineyard for the last time, that I may bring to pass my strange (wonderful) act, **that I may pour out my Spirit upon all flesh—**

Likewise, we read in Joel that the Lord will pour out His Spirit upon all flesh prior to the Second Coming of Christ. He said (bold added for emphasis):

Joel 2:28-29.

> 28 And it shall come to pass afterward, *that* **I will pour out my spirit upon all flesh**; and your sons and your daughters shall prophesy, your old men shall dream dreams, your young men shall see visions:
> 29 And also upon the servants and upon the handmaids **in those days will I pour out my spirit.**

So, what is the main message of this sign of the times? Answer: That in the last days, because of gross wickedness, great numbers of people will cease to feel the natural righteous emotions, feelings, common sense, wisdom, appreciation of beauty, nature, environment, worth of humans, etc. which are instilled and nourished by the Spirit. In place of these enlightened and enlightening attributes, they will be filled with the evil attributes and insensitivities listed by Paul in his warnings against wickedness found in several of his writings. We will consider two such references from his epistles here. First, 2 Timothy 3:1-7:

1 This know also, that in the last days perilous times shall come.

2 For men shall be lovers of their own selves, covetous, boasters, proud, blasphemers, disobedient to parents, unthankful, unholy,

3 Without natural affection, trucebreakers, false accusers, incontinent, fierce, despisers of those that are good,

4 Traitors, heady, highminded, lovers of pleasures more than lovers of God;

5 Having a form of godliness, but denying the power thereof: from such turn away.

6 For of this sort are they which creep into houses, and lead captive silly women laden with sins, led away with divers lusts,

7 Ever learning, and never able to come to the knowledge of the truth.

Paul gives a similar but expanded list in Romans 1:29-32 (with notes in parentheses taken from *The New Testament Made Easier, Part 2*, by David J. Ridges, Cedar Fort Inc., 2003).

29 Being filled with all unrighteousness (with all kinds of sins), fornication (sexual immorality), wickedness (depravity; see Strong's #4189), covetousness, maliciousness (meanness); full of envy, murder, debate (strife, arguing), deceit (dishonesty), malignity (plotting evil against others); whisperers (gossipers),

30 Backbiters (slanderers; people who ruin other peoples' reputations), haters of God, despiteful (violent, overbearing), proud, boasters, inventors of evil things (thinking up more ways to be wicked), disobedient to parents,

31 Without understanding (foolish, stupid; see Strong's # 0801), covenantbreakers, without natural affection (heartless), implacable (refuse to make covenants; see Strong's # 0786), unmerciful:

32 Who knowing the judgment of God (they are sinning against knowledge), that they which commit such things are worthy of death (They know God's commandments and that people who commit such sins will die spiritually and will eventually be cut off from God), not only do the same (they not only commit such sins), but have pleasure in them that do them (they approve of and encourage others to commit such sins). (In other words, members of the Church who have been taught the gospel and understand it, and still commit such sins, are very accountable. The effects on their spirituality are tragic. A major problem is that they not only commit such sins themselves, but they also encourage others to do the same.)

27. PEACE WILL BE TAKEN FROM THE EARTH.

Category: Being Fulfilled.

Again, as with the previous sign of the time, we must be careful to keep this sign in context. Obviously, peace is being taken from the earth. This sign is being fulfilled. There are wars and rumors of war. Violent civil wars rage on every hand. Gangs destroy the tranquility in once peaceful neighborhoods. Movies make millions by making violence exciting. Even much of music is about violence and is violent itself. Mass media makes violence available to the masses almost everywhere. In D&C 1:35, the Lord tells us (bold added for emphasis):

35 For I am no respecter of persons, and will that all men shall know that the day speedily cometh; the hour is not yet, but is nigh at hand, when **peace shall be taken from the earth**, and the devil shall have power over his own dominion.

As you can see in verse 35, above, when the Lord gave this revelation to Joseph Smith in 1831, He said "the hour is not yet, but is night at hand" when this sign would begin to be fulfilled. Surely, it is underway now. But we must remember also that when we try our best to do right, there is peace in our hearts. When there is peace in our hearts, there is peace on earth for us. Also, there is wonderful peace in living among the saints and in reading our scriptures and in creating righteous homes. In fact, the Lord provides great comfort in D&C 1:36 as follows (bold added for emphasis):

> 36 And also **the Lord shall have power over his saints**, and shall reign in their midst, and shall come down in judgment upon Idumea, or the world.

Furthermore, the Lord reminds us of the peace and safety to be had in the congregations of the members of the Church. In D&C 115:6, He said (bold added for emphasis):

Doctrine and Covenants 115:6.

> 6 And that the **gathering together** upon the land of Zion, and **upon her stakes**, may be **for a defense, and for a refuge from the storm**, and from wrath when it shall be poured out without mixture upon the whole earth.

When we read the above-quoted scriptures, we come to the conclusion that, in the final days prior to the Second Coming, peace will largely be taken from the earth and its inhabitants. However, when we listen carefully to President Hinckley's counsel about being happy, as in the following quote, we soon realize that we live in a marvelous age, and that there can be much of peace and beauty in our lives and in the world around us, when seen through the Gift of the Holy Ghost.

> *"I do not know what we did in the preexistence to merit the wonderful blessings we enjoy. We have come to earth in this*

great season in the long history of mankind. It is a marvelous age, the best of all. As we reflect on the plodding course of mankind, from the time of our first parents, we cannot help feeling grateful." (November 2001, Ensign.)

28. JERUSALEM WILL BE A "CUP OF TREMBLING" TO THOSE WHO ATTEMPT TO FIGHT AGAINST IT

Category: Fulfilled, Being Fulfilled.

This is one of the signs of the times which we can quite readily consider to be fulfilled. Israel has become a formidable military power, striking quickly and decisively against any who provoke its wrath. On the other hand, this prophecy continues being fulfilled on an almost daily basis. Therefore, we can go with either category on this one.

There is one caution which we should observe when it comes to this prophecy. Many are inclined to say that **all** nations will be against Israel in the last days. A more careful reading of several of the prophecies about nations who fight against Israel in the final scenes before the Second Coming can lead us to understand that all nations will be involved with Jerusalem (see heading to Zechariah, chapter 12 in our Bible). Thus, the prophecy that Jerusalem will be a "cup of trembling"applies to all nations who choose to fight against Israel. Lets look at some examples. First, Zechariah 12:2 (bold added for emphasis):

> 2 Behold, **I will make Jerusalem a cup of trembling unto all the people round about, when they shall be in the siege both against Judah *and* against Jerusalem.**

The wording in Zechariah 12:3 and 9 leads us to understand that verse two applies to nations who choose to fight against Israel. These verses read as follows (bold added for emphasis):

Zechariah 12:3.

> 3 And in that day will I make Jerusalem a burdensome stone for all people: all **that** burden themselves with it shall be cut in pieces, though all the people of the earth be gathered together against it.

Zechariah 12:9.

> 9 And it shall come to pass in that day, *that* I will seek to destroy all the nations **that** come against Jerusalem.

The world has seen and continues to see dramatic evidence of the fulfillment of this prophecy. From a rational standpoint, it would be absurd to think that such a tiny nation as Israel, a scant 40 miles wide and 140 miles long (this varies from time to time) could be the center of attention of the whole world and could wield military power which would intimidate much larger forces. As foretold by the Savior, in the following scripture reference, Israel has been trodden down by every nation who desired to do so for about 2,000 years (bold added for emphasis):

Luke 21:24

> 24 And they shall fall by the edge of the sword, and shall be led away captive into all nations: and **Jerusalem shall be trodden down of the Gentiles, until the times of the Gentiles be fulfilled.**

Israel today has indeed become a terror to any nations who attack it. It is indeed the fulfillment of prophecy. For instance, in June of 1967, during what is known as the "Six-Day War," Israeli soldiers defeated a much larger enemy force and, among other things, retook Jerusalem.

Another example of the fulfillment of this prophecy may be found in the "Raid on Entebbe." Early in July of 1976, my wife and I were in downtown Jerusalem climbing aboard a tour bus. We had noticed enthusiastic celebrating among people on the street, and asked our bus driver what was going on. He asked, "Haven't you heard?" We of course hadn't.

He went on to tell us of the rescue of Jewish hostages being held prisoners at the airport in Entebbe, Uganda, a rescue which had been completed that morning. According to him, a plane full of Jewish passengers had been commandeered by anti-Jewish terrorists who had taken them to Entebbe in Uganda, a country in eastern Africa. Having accomplished their deed, the terrorists mocked the nation of Israel and her citizens and made much political fodder out of the whole situation. Ultimately, the Jewish military determined to rescue the hostages.

They took three planes and flew the approximately 2,400 miles to Entebbe at night, flying so low as to be under radar range. They landed at the airport in Entebbe and took the hostages back after a brief firefight in which all but three or four hostages were saved. They quickly took off again and returned the beleaguered hostages to safety in Jerusalem. Such is the military status of Israel today. A prophecy fulfilled.

29. PEOPLE WILL REFUSE TO BELIEVE OBVIOUS TRUTH AND WILL INSTEAD ADHERE TO FABLES AND FALSEHOOD

Category: Being Fulfilled.

This prophecy of conditions shortly preceding the Second Coming of Christ needs little explanation. When people get sufficiently wicked and selfish, they no longer think rationally. Indeed, wickedness does not promote rational thought. In the face of social trends and political posturing which, to the rational mind, will obviously lead to the destruction of society as we know it, with its built-in safeguards for human freedom and use of agency, such people stand aghast at truth and moral principles. They flush in anger at those who advocate the standards of the Bible and the gospel of Christ as the basis for the survival of society. Paul, the Apostle, prophesied this stance in 2 Timothy 4:3-4, as follows. He said (bold added for emphasis):

> 3 For **the time will come when they will not endure sound doctrine**; but after their own lusts shall they heap to themselves teachers, having itching ears;
> 4 And **they shall turn away** *their* **ears from the truth, and shall be turned unto fables**.

We often apply these verses to the gospel and the tendency of the spiritually blind and deaf to reject its teachings and blessings. This is certainly the case. However, no doubt these verses can be applied also to common sense and rational thought processes in all matters relating to the governing of nations and communities as well as to standards to which the media should be held accountable.

The "teachers, having itching ears" and "fables" mentioned by Paul can certainly include the peers of those who would have us pass unrighteous or unwise laws, as well as the peers and fans of Hollywood and other media production centers who insist on the "anything goes" philosophy for entertainment.

30. FALSE PROPHETS, FALSE CHURCHES, AND FALSE MIRACLES ABOUND

Category: Being Fulfilled.

Speaking to His disciples about the last days, the Savior spoke of false Christs and false prophets and the false miracles which would be performed by them. He said (bold added for emphasis):

Joseph Smith–Matthew 1:22.

> 22 For in those days there shall also arise **false Christs**, and **false prophets**, and **shall show great signs and wonders**, insomuch, that, if possible, they shall deceive the very elect, who are the elect according to the covenant.

John the Revelator likewise prophesied such things in the last days. He referred to the great power of Satan and his "front" organizations to do spectacular things to attract the foolish, the unwary, and the wicked in the last days (bold added for emphasis):

Revelation 13:13-15.

> 13 And **he doeth great wonders,** so that **he maketh fire come down from heaven** on the earth **in the sight of men,** (Making "fire come down from heaven" is a reference to Elijah's miracle recorded in 1 Kings, chapter 18, where he challenged 450 prophets of Baal to have their god light the fire for their sacrifice. When they failed, God sent fire down from heaven to burn Elijah's offering. In other words, Satan and his followers can do spectacular things to woo their victims.)
>
> 14 And **deceiveth them that dwell on the earth by *the means of* those miracles** which **he had power to do** in the sight of the beast; saying to them that dwell on the earth, that they should make an image to the beast, which had the wound by a sword, and did live.
>
> 15 And **he had power to give life unto the image of the beast** (had power to make sin look very attractive), that the image of the beast should both speak, and cause that as many as would not worship the image of the beast should be killed.

Sometimes we tend to think of these false Christs and false prophets as well as false miracles only in terms of strange people dressed in long robes, or some televangelists, or false healings etc. While such people and events can certainly fit this prophecy, it may be a bit too narrow of an interpretation. Media idols, liberal philosophies, corrupt politicians and business people, and a host of other public and private heroes could well fit into this category. In fact, any in positions of influence who lead others astray could be considered to be in the category of false prophets and false Christs.

31. PEOPLE REFUSE TO BELIEVE THE SIGNS OF THE TIMES

Category: Being Fulfilled.

It is rather interesting to note that, according to Peter, one of the signs of the times is that people will refuse to even believe the signs of the times. People will be so far removed from God in their lifestyles and in their thinking that they will pay no attention to the obvious fulfillment of prophecy. In fact, they will scoff and say that things are just the same as ever and there is no such thing as "the last days." In 2 Peter 3:3-4, we read (bold added for emphasis):

> 3 Knowing this first, that there shall come **in the last days scoffers**, walking after their own lusts,
>
> 4 And **saying, Where is the promise of his coming?** for since the fathers fell asleep, **all things continue as *they were* from the beginning of the creation.**

32. THERE WILL BE SIGNS AND WONDERS ON EARTH AND IN THE HEAVENS

Category: Being Fulfilled.

Before the Savior's ascension into heaven, He spoke to His disciples about His Second Coming. He related a parable to them which told how signs of the times on earth and in the heavens would alert the faithful in the last days that His coming was near. Among other places, we read these words in D&C 45:36-40 as follows (bold added for emphasis):

> 36 And when the light shall begin to break forth, it shall be with them like unto **a parable** which I will show you—

37 Ye look and behold the fig-trees, and ye see them with your eyes, and ye say when they begin to shoot forth, and their leaves are yet tender, that summer is now nigh at hand;

38 Even so it shall be in that day **when they shall see all these things** (the signs of the times), **then shall they know that the hour is nigh.**

39 And it shall come to pass that he that feareth me shall be looking forth for the great day of the Lord to come, even for **the signs of the coming of the Son of Man**.

40 And **they shall see signs and wonders**, for they shall be shown forth **in the heavens above**, and **in the earth beneath**.

Perhaps many of the things which we take for granted in our day, such as airplanes, trains, rocket ships, space stations, satellites, automobiles, busses, computers, etc. would serve as astonishing "signs and wonders" to all who have lived on the earth prior to these last days.

33. THE LAMANITES WILL BLOSSOM AS THE ROSE

Category: Being Fulfilled.

This much-anticipated sign of the times is certainly taking place on a broad scale right before our eyes. It is spoken of in D&C 49:24 and reads as follows (bold added for emphasis):

24 But **before the great day of the Lord shall come**, Jacob shall flourish in the wilderness, and **the Lamanites shall blossom as the rose**.

All four of our sons served missions to South America and witnessed first hand the ongoing fulfilling of this prophecy. On every hand we observe the continued rapid growth of the Church among our Lamanite brothers and sisters.

The Perpetual Education Fund, instituted by President Gordon B. Hinckley, is being implemented on a large scale among returned missionaries in Mexico, Central and South America. This, no doubt, is helping also to fulfill this sign of the times, for it helps them not only to "blossom" in terms of membership in the Lord's true Church, but it also helps them to "blossom" and flourish in terms of economic well-being.

34. NEW JERUSALEM WILL BE BUILT

Category: Yet Future.

Before the Lord's Second Advent, the city of New Jerusalem will be built in Independence, Jackson County, Missouri. This "Holy City" (Moses 7:62) is often referred to as the "city of Zion" (D&C 57:2) and will continue on into the Millennium, serving as one of two capital cities for the Savior during the Millennium. The other capital city will be Old Jerusalem.

The location of the city of Zion or New Jerusalem is given in D&C 57:1-3 as follows (bold added for emphasis):

> 1 Hearken, O ye elders of my church, saith the Lord your God, who have assembled yourselves together, according to my commandments, in this land, which is **the land of Missouri**, which is the land which I have appointed and consecrated for the gathering of the saints.
>
> 2 Wherefore, **this is** the land of promise, and **the place for the city of Zion**.
>
> 3 And thus saith the Lord your God, if you will receive wisdom here is wisdom. Behold, the place which is now called **Independence is the center place**; and a spot for the temple is lying westward, upon a lot which is not far from the courthouse.

More detail about New Jerusalem is given in D&C 45:66-69 as follows (bold added for emphasis):

66 And **it shall be called the New Jerusalem**, a land
of peace, a city of refuge, **a place of safety** for the
saints of the Most High God;

67 And **the glory of the Lord shall be there**, and the
terror of the Lord also shall be there, insomuch that **the
wicked will not come unto it**, and it shall be called
Zion.

68 And it shall come to pass among the wicked, that
**every man that will not take his sword against his
neighbor must needs flee unto Zion for safety**.

69 And **there shall be gathered unto it out of every
nation under heaven**; and it shall be **the only
people that shall not be at war one with another**.

We are given more information about this Holy City in
Moses 7:62-64, including the fact that the Savior will live there
during the Millennium. These verses follow (bold added for
emphasis):

62 And righteousness will I send down out of heaven;
and truth will I send forth out of the earth, to bear
testimony of mine Only Begotten; his resurrection
from the dead; yea, and also the resurrection of all men;
and righteousness and truth will I cause to sweep the
earth as with a flood, to **gather out mine elect** from
the four quarters of the earth, **unto a place which I
shall prepare, an Holy City, that my people may**
gird up their loins, and **be looking forth for the
time of my coming**; for there shall be my tabernacle,
and **it shall be called Zion, a New Jerusalem**.

63 And the Lord said unto **Enoch**: Then shalt thou **and
all thy city meet them there**, and we will receive
them into our bosom, and they shall see us; and we will
fall upon their necks, and they shall fall upon our necks,
and we will kiss each other;

64 And there shall be **mine abode**, and it shall be Zion,
which shall come forth out of all the creations which I

have made; and **for the space of a thousand years** the earth shall rest.

We mentioned above that Old Jerusalem would also become a capital city for the Savior during the Millennium. Old Jerusalem will be built up again and will become "a holy city of the Lord" as prophesied in Ether 13:5-6 as follows (bold added for emphasis):

> 5 And he spake also concerning the house of Israel, and **the Jerusalem from whence Lehi should come—** after it should be destroyed it **should be built up again, a holy city unto the Lord**; wherefore, it could not be a new Jerusalem for it had been in a time of old; but it should be built up again, and become a holy city of the Lord; and it should be built unto the house of Israel.
>
> 6 And that **a New Jerusalem should be built up upon this land**, unto the remnant of the seed of Joseph, for which things there has been a type.

Joseph Fielding Smith explained the above verses as follows:

> *"These two cities, one in the land of Zion and one in Palestine, are to become capitals for the kingdom of God during the Millennium."* (Doctrines of Salvation, *Vol. 3, page 71.)*

In summary, while there is much more which could be said about New Jerusalem, suffice it to say that the Building of New Jerusalem is yet future. It will be built, at least in part, before the Second Coming, and, according to Moses 7:62 as quoted above, the inhabitants of it will be "looking forth for the time of my coming" and will have a safe haven during the ravages of the last of the final days before the Lord's Coming.

35. MANY TEMPLES WILL BE BUILT

Category: Being Fulfilled.

In the last days, before the Coming of the Lord, the inhabitants of the earth are to have numerous temples available to them. In the April, 1980, General Conference of the Church, Ezra Taft Benson prophesied that we would someday have temples in all the lands where the gospel has penetrated. He said (bold added for emphasis):

> *"But now—what of the future? We assuredly expect additional progress, growth, and increased spirituality. We will see our missionaries cover the earth with the message of the Restoration.* ***We will see temples in every land where the gospel has penetrated,*** *symbolizing the truth that families, living and deceased, may be joined together in love and eternal family associations." (Ezra Taft Benson, "A Marvelous Work and a Wonder,"* Ensign, May 1980, 33.)

The word "mountain" is often used in the scriptures to symbolize "temple." Thus, the phrase "mountain of the Lord's house" in Isaiah's prophecy of the last days in Isaiah 2:2 can refer not only to the establishment of the Church in the tops of the mountains in the last days, but also to temples. The phrase "mountains (note that this is plural) of the Lord's house" in D&C 133:13 can mean "temples." Both verses are given next, with bold added for emphasis:

Isaiah 2:2.

> 2 And it shall come to pass in the last days, *that* **the mountain of the LORD's house shall be established in the top of the mountains**, and shall be exalted above the hills; and all nations shall flow unto it.

Doctrine and Covenants 133:13.

13 And let them who be of Judah flee unto Jerusalem,
unto the mountains of the Lord's house.

Thus, it was prophesied by Isaiah and by the Prophet Joseph
Smith that, in the last days, temples would once more be available. This interpretation of this phrase is summarized in the
Institute of Religion *Doctrine and Covenants Student Manual*, page
339, as follows (bold added for emphasis):

D&C 133:13. What Does the Phrase "Mountains of the Lord's House" Mean?

Other Church leaders have also taught about "the
mountain of the Lord's house." Elder Erastus Snow said:
"'The mountain of the Lord's house' — this is a pecu-
liar phrase, and was probably used by the Prophet
because it was a common mode of expression in Israel
in the days of David and many of the Prophets several
hundred years after him, for, in **speaking of Mount
Moriah, on which the Temple of Solomon was
built**, they spoke of it as the mountain of the Lord's
house. Moriah is a hill in the city of Jerusalem, on
which David located the site of the Temple, and on
which his son Solomon built it, and it was called the
mountain of the house of the Lord." (In Journal of
Discourses, 16:202.)

Elder Bruce R. McConkie explained that the phrase
has more than one meaning: "The mountain of the
Lord's house is the mountain where the temple of God
is built. [Isaiah 2:2-3 quoted; see also Micah 4:1-2; 2
Nephi 12:2-3.] "This great prophecy, as is often the
case, is subject to the law of multiple fulfillment. 1. In
Salt Lake City and other mountain locations temples, in
the full and true sense of the word, have been erected,

and representatives of all nations are flowing unto them to learn of God and his ways.... 2. But the day is yet future when the Lord's house is to be built on that 'Mount Zion' which is 'the city of New Jerusalem' in Jackson County, Missouri. (D. & C. 84:2-4.) Mount Zion, itself, will be the mountain of the Lord's house in the day when that glorious temple is erected. 3. When the Jews flee unto Jerusalem, it will be 'unto the mountains of the Lord's house' (D. & C. 133:13), for a holy temple is to be built there also as part of the work of the great era of restoration. (Ezek. 37:24-28.)" [*Doctrine and Covenants Student Manual*, p.339.]

36. A TEMPLE WILL BE BUILT IN JERUSALEM

Category: Yet Future.

Many questions are asked by members of the Church about this temple which is yet to be built and which is a very prominent sign of the times. We will pose just a few questions and give answers:

Question: Will this temple be built on the Dome of the Rock?

Answer: This is a most unfortunate rumor because it causes additional animosity between Christians and Muslims. There is nowhere in the scriptures where it is stated that the Jerusalem Temple has to be built on the exact site of the Dome of the Rock, a mosque which is so sacred to Muslims. There is actually plenty of room on the so called "Temple Mount" for both.

Question: Is it possible that the BYU Jerusalem Center could be turned into a temple?

Answer: The Brethren are very concerned about this

unfounded rumor and have actually asked seminary and institute of religion teachers to do everything they can to stop it from spreading. The Brethren gave their word to the Israeli government that the Jerusalem Center is an educational center, and so it is. To do otherwise with it would be a breach of promise.

Question: Will this temple be one in which temple ordinances will be performed?

Answer: Yes. Joseph Fielding Smith answers this question as follows:

> *"**LATTER-DAY TEMPLES FORETOLD.** That temples and temple ordinances are essential to the Christian faith is well established in the Bible. Malachi predicted the coming of the Lord suddenly to his temple, in the day of vengeance, in the latter times, as a refiner and purifier. Ezekiel predicted the building of a **temple in Jerusalem which will be used for ordinance work** after the gathering of Israel from their long dispersion and when they are cleansed from their transgressions."* (Joseph Fielding Smith, Doctrines of Salvation, 3 vols., edited by Bruce R. McConkie [Salt Lake City: Bookcraft, 1954-1956], 2: 244.)

The Prophet Joseph Smith spoke of the temple which is to be built in Jerusalem. He said (bold added for emphasis):

> *Judah must return, **Jerusalem must be rebuilt, and the temple**, and water come out from under the temple, and the waters of the Dead Sea be healed. It will take some time to rebuild the walls of the city and the temple, etc.; and **all this must be done before the Son of Man will make His appearance.** (April 6, 1843.)* (Joseph Smith, Teachings of the Prophet Joseph Smith, selected and arranged by Joseph Fielding Smith [Salt Lake City: Deseret Book Co., 1976], page 286.)

37. THE RAINBOW IS WITHDRAWN

Category: ?

The Prophet Joseph Smith gave what has become known to some as "the rainbow prophecy." It is as follows (bold added for emphasis):

> "*I have asked of the Lord concerning His coming; and while asking the Lord, He gave a sign and said, 'In the days of Noah I set a bow in the heavens as a sign and token that **in any year that the bow should be seen the Lord would not come**; but there should be seed time and harvest during that year: but **whenever you see the bow withdrawn**, it shall be a token that there shall be famine, pestilence, and great distress among the nations, and that **the coming of the Messiah is not far distant**.' (Joseph Smith,* History of The Church of Jesus Christ of Latter-day Saints, *7 vols., introduction and notes by B. H. Roberts [Salt Lake City: The Church of Jesus Christ of Latter-day Saints, 1932-1951], Vol. 6, page 254.)*

Until we receive more information from an authorized source, we are left to wonder what category this prophecy should be placed in. Some people ask if it means that there would be absolutely no rainbows, not even in sprinkler systems or in small waterfalls. Most prophecies do not lend themselves to such extremes. We will simply have to wait for additional revelation on this one.

38. THE CONSTITUTION WILL HANG BY A THREAD

Category: Being Fulfilled.

In our day, it seems that we are watching the Constitution being unraveled. But it is not so much that the actual wording of the Constitution is being changed. Rather, the intent and meaning of the founding fathers is being reinterpreted by the courts of our land, thus rendering their inspired intent and wording ineffective.

The Lord established the Constitution of the United States of America by the hands of the founding fathers. These were wise and inspired men who were sent to earth and positioned by the Lord for this exact purpose. In D&C 101:77-80, we read (bold added for emphasis):

> 77 According to **the** laws and **constitution** of the people, **which I have suffered to be established,** and should be maintained for the rights and protection of all flesh, according to just and holy principles;
>
> 78 **That every man may act** in doctrine and principle pertaining to futurity, **according to** the **moral agency** which I have given unto him, **that every man may be accountable for his own sins** in the day of judgment.
>
> 79 Therefore, it is not right that any man should be in bondage one to another.
>
> 80 And for this purpose have **I established the Constitution of this land, by the hands of wise men whom I raised up unto this very purpose,** and redeemed the land by the shedding of blood.

Brigham Young was one of a number who prophesied that the day would come that the Constitution would hang by a thread. But he also said that it would not be destroyed. It will be saved by members of the Church. He said:

> *"Will the Constitution be destroyed: No: it will be held inviolate by this people; and, as Joseph Smith said, 'The time will come when the destiny of the nation will hang upon a single thread. At that critical juncture, this people will step forth and save it from the threatened destruction.' It will be so." (Journal of Discourses, Vol. 7, page 15.)*

"When the Constitution of the United States hangs, as it were, upon a single thread, they will have to call for the 'Mormon" elders to save it from utter destruction; and they will step forth and do it." (Journal of Discourses, *Vol. 2, page 182.)*

39. DESTROYING ANGELS WILL BE ALLOWED TO GO FORTH UPON THE EARTH

Category: Being Fulfilled.

In D&C 8:5-6, the Lord told the early saints of this dispensation that angels even at that time were asking for permission to go forth and begin to harvest the tares (the wicked). We read (bold added for emphasis):

5 Behold, verily I say unto you, **the angels are crying unto the Lord day and night**, who are ready and waiting **to be sent forth to reap down the fields**;
6 **But the Lord saith** unto them, **pluck not up the tares** while the blade is yet tender (for verily your faith is weak), **lest you destroy the wheat also.**

President Wilford Woodruff told members of the Church that these angels have now been loosed and are going forth upon the earth. He said:

"What is the matter with the world today? What has created this change that we see coming over the world? Why these terrible earthquakes, tornados, and judgments? What is the meaning of all these mighty events that are taking place? The meaning is, these angels that have been held for many years in the temple of our God [in heaven] have got their liberty to go out and commence their mission and their work in the earth, and they are here today in the earth." (The Young Woman's Journal, *Vol. 56, page 643. October 8, 1894.)*

40. THE "ABOMINATION OF DESOLATION" WILL HAPPEN AGAIN

Category: Being Fulfilled.

The reason we would suggest that this prophecy is being fulfilled is that, in the Bible Dictionary in the back of our Bible, it explains this sign, as far as the last days are concerned, as "Jerusalem again will be under siege." (See Bible Dictionary, page 601, under Abomination of Desolation.) Jerusalem is certainly "under siege" today and has been for years.

This is one of the signs of the times spoken of, among other places, in Joseph Smith–Matthew, 1:32, wherein we are told that this prophecy will be fulfilled in the last days before the Savior Comes. We read (bold added for emphasis):

32 And **again** shall the **abomination of desolation**, spoken of by Daniel the prophet, be fulfilled.

It is also mentioned in Matthew 24:15 as follows (bold added for emphasis):

15 When ye therefore shall see the **abomination of desolation**, spoken of by Daniel the prophet, stand in the holy place, (whoso readeth, let him understand:)

For an explanation of the phrase "abomination of desolation," we will turn to the Institute of Religion Student Manual, entitled, *The Life and Teachings of Jesus and His Apostles*, page 152, as follows (bold added for emphasis):

Matthew 24:15-22. 29, 34, 35. What Is the Abomination of Desolation Spoken of by Daniel the Prophet and the Savior?

There were to be **two times** when this great tragedy would occur:

1. To the Jews at Jerusalem.

"And now the ax was laid at the root of the rotted tree. Jerusalem was to pay the price. Daniel had foretold this hour when desolation, **born of abomination and wickedness,** would sweep the city. (Dan. 9:27; 11:31; 12:11.) Moses had said the siege would be so severe women would eat their own children. (Deut. 28.) Jesus specified the destruction would come in the days of the disciples.

"And come it did, in vengeance, without restraint. Hunger exceeded human endurance; blood flowed in the streets; destruction made desolate the temple; 1,100,000 Jews were slaughtered; Jerusalem was ploughed as a field; and a remnant of a once mighty nation was scattered to the ends of the earth. The Jewish nation died, impaled on Roman spears, at the hands of Gentile overlords.

"**But what of the saints who dwelt in Jerusalem in that gloomy day? They heeded Jesus' warning and fled in haste. Guided by revelation, as true saints always are, they fled to Pella in Perea and were spared.**" (McConkie, *DNTC*, 1:644-45.)

2. At the Time of the Second Coming.

"All the desolation and waste which attended the former destruction of Jerusalem is but prelude to the coming siege. Titus and his legions slaughtered 1,100,000 Jews, destroyed the temple, and ploughed the city. **In the coming reenactment of this 'abomination of desolation,' the whole world will be at war,** Jerusalem will be the center of the conflict, every modern weapon will be used, and in the midst of the siege the Son of Man shall come, setting his foot upon the mount of Olives and fighting the battle of his saints. (Zech. 12:1-9.)

"Speaking of these final battles which shall accompany his return, the Lord says: `I will gather all nations against Jerusalem to battle; and the city shall be taken, and the houses rifled, and the women ravished; and half of the city shall go forth into captivity, and the residue of the people shall not be cut off from the city.' However, the final end of the conflict shall be different this time than it was anciently. `Then shall the Lord go forth,' the prophetic record says, `and fight against those nations, as when he fought in the day of battle. And his feet shall stand in that day upon the mount of Olives, ... and the Lord shall be king over all the earth.' (Zech. 14.)" (McConkie, DNTC; 1:659-60.)

As mentioned above, in the Bible Dictionary in our Bible, page 601, we also read about these two fulfillments of the "abomination of desolation." Speaking of the one to occur in the last days before the Coming of Christ, we read (bold added for emphasis):

> "Speaking of **the last days,** of the days following the restoration of the gospel and its declaration 'for a witness unto all nations,' our Lord said: 'And again shall the abomination of desolation, spoken of by Daniel the prophet, be fulfilled' (JS–M 1:31-32). That is, **Jerusalem again will be under siege.**" (Bible Dictionary, page 601.)

41. WICKEDNESS WILL BE RAMPANT
Category: Being Fulfilled.

While this sign of the times may be considered a summary of several of the signs of the times already given previously in this book, it merits being discussed as a sign in and of itself. It appears that wickedness in the last days prior to the Second Advent of Christ won't just "happen" as a matter of natural deterioration of morals and values. Rather, if we understand this prophecy correctly, it will be the direct result of wickedness spread intentionally by use of mass media which will cause an unprecedented acceleration of evil and virtual "free fall" of society. Satan will be at the helm of this "desolating scourge" of wickedness. Nephi warns of Satan's devastating power in the last days as follows (bold added for emphasis):

2 Nephi 28:20.

> 20 For behold, **at that day shall he rage in the hearts of the children of men,** and stir them up to anger against that which is good.

42. BABYLON WILL FALL

Category: Yet Future.

"**Babylon**" may be basically defined as "Satan's kingdom." All who follow his wicked and evil ways are "citizens of Babylon." Obviously, Babylon has not yet fallen. Therefore, the fulfillment of this sign is yet future. This prophecy seems to be divided into **two categories. First,** many of the wicked will fall before the actual Coming of Christ. **Second,** those who remain will be destroyed by the Lord when He actually comes. We read about this in Revelation 19:17-21. In verse 21, we see that the wicked who survived the terrible battles among the wicked in the final stages of the earth, are destroyed "with the sword of him that sat upon the horse" or Christ (see Revelation 19:11). These verses read as follows (bold added for emphasis):

Revelation 19:17-21.

> 17 And I saw an angel standing in the sun; and he cried with a loud voice, saying to all the fowls that fly in the

midst of heaven, Come and gather yourselves together unto the supper of the great God;

18 That ye may eat the flesh of kings, and the flesh of captains, and the flesh of mighty men, and the flesh of horses, and of them that sit on them, and the flesh of all *men, both* free and bond, both small and great.

19 And I saw the beast, and the **kings of the earth, and their armies, gathered together to make war against him that sat on the horse, and against his army**.

20 And the beast was taken, and with him the false prophet that wrought miracles before him, with which he deceived them that had received the mark of the beast, and them that worshipped his image. These both were cast alive into a lake of fire burning with brimstone.

21 And the **remnant** were **slain with the sword of him that sat upon the horse**, which *sword* proceeded out of his mouth: and all the fowls were filled with their flesh.

"Babylon" has many names in the scriptures. Two of these names are used in D&C 29:21 in referring to the final fall of Satan's kingdom before the Millennium. They are "the great and abominable church" and "the whore of all the earth." These are very strong terms and are a reminder of how evil Lucifer and his wicked hosts are. D&C 29:21 reads as follows (bold added for emphasis):

21 And **the great and abominable church**, which is **the whore of all the earth, shall be cast down** by devouring fire, according as it is spoken by the mouth of Ezekiel the prophet, who spoke of these things, which have not come to pass but surely must, as I live, for abominations shall not reign.

43. A GREAT HAILSTORM WILL DESTROY THE CROPS OF THE EARTH

Category: Yet Future.

All we know about this sign of the times is that the Lord said that it would happen in the last days before His coming. In D&C 29:16, we read (bold added for emphasis):

16 And there shall be **a great hailstorm sent forth to destroy the crops of the earth**.

We find another reference to hail as a sign of the times in the Book of revelation. In this reference, it indicates that there will damage to people as a result. Revelation 16:21 says (bold added for emphasis):

21 And **there fell upon men a great hail** out of heaven, every stone about the weight of a talent: and men blasphemed God because of the plague of the hail; for the plague thereof was exceeding great.

It is interesting to wonder how heavy a "talent" is, as used in verse 21 above. We really don't know (see Bible Dictionary, page 789, under *talent* in our Bible.) On occasions someone will use the Old Testament system of weights in which a talent would be the equivalent of about 75 pounds, and thus they describe these hailstones which "fell upon men" as being in the neighborhood of 75 pounds each. The problem with this is that the New Testament system of weights is not the same as the Old Testament system. Therefore, we are left to understand simply that a devastating hailstorm will be one of the signs of the times when gross wickedness dominates the earth.

44. THERE WILL BE A GREAT EARTH-QUAKE SUCH AS NEVER BEFORE

Category: Yet Future.

This, too, is a sign of the times for which we have very little information. In Revelation 16:18 it says (bold added for emphasis):

> 18 And there were voices, and thunders, and lightnings; and there was **a great earthquake, such as was not since men were upon the earth,** so mighty an earthquake, and so great.

Another reference to this monumental event is found in Revelation 6:12 as follows (bold added for emphasis):

> 12 And I beheld when he had opened the sixth seal, and, lo, there was **a great earthquake;** and the sun became black as sackcloth of hair, and the moon became as blood;

45. THE BATTLE OF ARMAGEDDON

Category: Yet Future.

This will be a tremendous battle, focused against the Jews in the Holy Land and signaled by an unprecedented siege against Jerusalem. All nations of the earth will be involved in it, whether fighting against the Jews or fighting for them. Sometimes this battle is also called the battle of Gog and Magog. Joseph Fielding Smith clarified these terms as follows (bold added for emphasis):

> *"**Before the coming of Christ,** the great war, sometimes called **Armageddon,** will take place as spoken of by Ezekiel, chapters 38 and 39. Another war of **Gog and Magog will be after the millennium."** (Joseph Fielding Smith,* Doctrines of Salvation, *3 vols., edited by Bruce R. McConkie [Salt Lake City: Bookcraft, 1954-1956], 3: 45.)*

Speaking of the final scenes before the Coming of the Lord, John the Revelator describes what he saw in vision, including reference to the final great battle in a place called "Armageddon". This is recorded in Revelation 16:14-16 as follows (bold added for emphasis):

14 For they are the spirits of devils, working miracles, *which* go forth unto the kings of the earth and of the whole world, **to gather them to the battle of that great day of God Almighty.**

15 Behold, I come as a thief. Blessed *is* he that watcheth, and keepeth his garments, lest he walk naked, and they see his shame.

16 And **he gathered them together into a place called** in the Hebrew tongue **Armageddon.**

You may wish to read a bit more about Armageddon in the Bible Dictionary, page 614 in our Bible. It refers to Zechariah, chapters 11 to 14 which have considerable prophecy about these final scenes. For instance, Zechariah 12:2-9 speaks of the Savior's saving the Jews against all nations who choose to fight against them, as follows (bold added for emphasis):

2 Behold, I will make Jerusalem a cup of trembling unto all the people round about, **when they shall be in the siege both against Judah *and* against Jerusalem**.

3 ¶ And in that day will I make Jerusalem a burdensome stone for all people: **all that burden themselves with it shall be cut in pieces**, though all the people of the earth be gathered together against it.

4 In that day, saith the LORD, I will smite every horse (symbolic of military power) with astonishment, and his rider with madness: and I will open mine eyes upon the house of Judah, and will smite every horse of the people with blindness.

5 And the governors of Judah shall say in their heart, The inhabitants of Jerusalem *shall be* my strength in the

LORD of hosts their God.

6 In that day will I make the governors of Judah like an hearth of fire among the wood, and like a torch of fire in a sheaf; and they shall devour all the people round about, on the right hand and on the left: and **Jerusalem shall be inhabited again in her own place,** *even* **in Jerusalem.**

7 **The LORD also shall save the tents of Judah** first, that the glory of the house of David and the glory of the inhabitants of Jerusalem do not magnify *themselves* against Judah.

8 **In that day shall the LORD defend the inhabitants of Jerusalem**; and he that is feeble among them at that day shall be as David; and the house of David *shall be* as God, as the angel of the LORD before them.

9 ¶ And it shall come to pass **in that day,** *that* **I will seek to destroy all the nations that come against Jerusalem.**

One caution, as counseled by several of the Brethren. We would do well not to make each of the battles in the Holy Land into **the** Battle of Armageddon in our minds. Certainly they are leading up to it and we would be wise to look at them with a knowing eye, being aware of the prophecies about Armageddon. But we should leave it to our prophets to alert us when the actual Battle of Armageddon begins taking place.

Just one last note about the location of the valley of Armageddon which is known today as the valley of Megiddo. This quote is taken from the Bible Dictionary, page 614:

"The valley of Megiddo is in the western portion of the plain of Esdraelon 50 miles north of Jerusalem."

46. THE MEETING AT ADAM-ONDI-AHMAN

Category: Yet Future.

Prior to the actual Second Coming, a large meeting will be held in Adam-ondi-Ahman, which is located in the state of Missouri, about 70 miles northeast of Independence (see map on page 297 at the end of the Doctrine and Covenants.) We will discuss who will attend in a moment, but first, some background as to the historic and sacred nature of this beautiful area. When Adam was 927 years old, he gathered his posterity together for a final meeting with them in Adam-ondi-Ahman. We read of this in D&C 107:53-57 as follows (bold added for emphasis):

53 **Three years previous to the death of Adam, he called** Seth, Enos, Cainan, Mahalaleel, Jared, Enoch, and Methuselah, who were all high priests, with **the residue of his posterity who were righteous, into the valley of Adam-ondi-Ahman,** and there bestowed upon them his last blessing.

54 **And the Lord appeared** unto them, and they rose up and blessed Adam, and called him Michael, the prince, the archangel.

55 And **the Lord administered comfort unto Adam,** and said unto him: I have set thee to be at the head; a multitude of nations shall come of thee, and thou art a prince over them forever.

56 And **Adam stood up** in the midst of the congregation; **and,** notwithstanding he was bowed down with age, being full of the Holy Ghost, **predicted whatsoever should befall his posterity unto the latest generation.**

57 These things were **all written in the book of Enoch,** and are to be testified of in due time.

We are told in Doctrine and Covenants, section 116, as well as in Daniel 7:9-14, that Adam will once again meet with his righteous posterity who will honor him prior to the Second Coming. The Savior will also attend this gathering. In D&C 116, we read:

> 1 Spring Hill is named by the Lord Adam-ondi-Ahman, because, said he, it is the place where Adam shall come to visit his people, or the Ancient of Days shall sit, as spoken of by Daniel the prophet.

This will be a rather large gathering, as you will see in the next quote. In Daniel 7:9-14, we read (bold added for emphasis plus some explanatory notes in parentheses):

> 9 I (Daniel) beheld till the thrones were cast down (in the last days), and **the Ancient of days** (Adam) did sit, whose garment *was* white as snow, and the hair of his head like the pure wool: his throne *was like* the fiery flame, *and* his wheels *as* burning fire.
>
> 10 A fiery stream issued and came forth from before him: **thousand thousands** (millions) ministered unto him, and **ten thousand times ten thousand** (a hundred million) stood before him: the judgment was set, and the books were opened.
>
> 11 I beheld then because of the voice of the great words which the horn spake: I beheld *even* till the beast was slain, and his body destroyed, and given to the burning flame.
>
> 12 As concerning the rest of the beasts, they had their dominion taken away: yet their lives were prolonged for a season and time.
>
> 13 I (Daniel) saw in the night visions, and, behold, *one* like **the Son of man** (Christ) came with the clouds of heaven, and **came to the Ancient of days** (Adam), and they brought him (Adam) near before him (Christ).

14 And **there was given** him (Christ) **dominion, and glory, and a kingdom, that all people, nations, and languages, should serve him** (the Millennium): his dominion *is* an everlasting dominion, which shall not pass away, and his kingdom *that* which shall not be destroyed.

We learn from the above quote that the meeting at Adam-ondi-Ahman, before the actual Second Coming, will be a rather large gathering, where Adam will gather his righteous posterity together. Christ will come also and those present, in authority, will turn their keys of power over to Him to use as He ushers in the Millennium.

Bruce R. McConkie gives additional explanation about what takes place at this gathering as follows:

"Before the Lord Jesus descends openly and publicly in the clouds of glory, attended by all the hosts of heaven; before the great and dreadful day of the Lord sends terror and destruction from one end of the earth to the other; before he stands on Mount Zion, or sets his feet on Olivet, or utters his voice from an American Zion or a Jewish Jerusalem; before all flesh shall see him together; before any of his appearances, which taken together comprise the Second Coming of the Son of God— before all these, there is to be a secret appearance to selected members of his Church. He will come in private to his prophet and to the apostles then living. Those who have held keys and powers and authorities in all ages from Adam to the present will also be present. And further, all the faithful members of the Church then living and all the faithful saints of all the ages past will be present. It will be the greatest congregation of faithful saints ever assembled on planet earth. It will be a sacrament meeting. It will be a day of judgment for the faithful of all the ages. And it will take place in Daviess County,

Missouri, at a place called Adam-ondi-Ahman." (Bruce R. McConkie, The Millennial Messiah: The Second Coming of the Son of Man *[Salt Lake City: Deseret Book Co., 1982], 578.)*

"With reference to the use of sacramental wine in our day, the Lord said to Joseph Smith: 'You shall partake of none except it is made new among you; yea, in this my Father's kingdom which shall be built up on the earth.' In so stating, he is picking up the language he used in the upper room. Then he says: 'The hour cometh that I will drink of the fruit of the vine with you on the earth.' Jesus is going to partake of the sacrament again with his mortal disciples on earth. But it will not be with mortals only. He names others who will be present and who will participate in the sacred ordinance. These include Moroni, Elias, John the Baptist, Elijah, Abraham, Isaac, Jacob, Joseph (who was sold into Egypt), Peter, James, and John, 'and also with Michael, or Adam, the father of all, the prince of all, the ancient of days.' Each of these is named simply by way of illustration. The grand summation of the whole matter comes in these words: 'And also with all those whom my Father hath given me out of the world.' (D&C 27:4-14.) The sacrament is to be administered in a future day, on this earth, when the Lord Jesus is present, and when all the righteous of all ages are present. This, of course, will be a part of the grand council at Adam-ondi-Ahman.

"Adam-ondi-Ahman—meaning the place or land of God where Adam dwelt—is at a place called Spring Hill, Daviess County, Missouri. This site is named by the Lord 'Adam-ondi-Ahman, because, said he, it is the place where Adam shall come to visit his people, or the Ancient of Days shall sit, as spoken of by Daniel the prophet.' (D&C 116.) There is a great valley there in which the righteous will assemble; and where there are valleys, the surrounding elevations are called

mountains. Thus our revelations speak of 'the mountains of Adam-ondi-Ahman' and of 'the plains of Olaha Shinehah, or the land where Adam dwelt.' (D&C 117:8.) Sacred indeed is the whole region for what has taken place and what will take place in its environs." (Bruce R. McConkie, The Millennial Messiah: The Second Coming of the Son of Man [Salt Lake City: Deseret Book Co., 1982], 587.)

We will use a quote from the Prophet Joseph Smith as a final summary for this particular sign of the times:

"Daniel in his seventh chapter speaks of the Ancient of Days; he means the oldest man, our Father Adam, Michael, he [who] will call his children together and hold a council with them to prepare them for the coming of the Son of Man. He (Adam) is the father of the human family, and presides over the spirits of all men, and all that have had the keys must stand before him in this grand council. This may take place before some of us leave this stage of action. The Son of Man stands before him, and there is given him glory and dominion. Adam delivers up his stewardship to Christ, that which was delivered to him as holding the keys of the universe, but retains his standing as head of the human family." (Joseph Smith, Teachings of the Prophet Joseph Smith, p. 157.)

47. TWO PROPHETS WILL BE KILLED IN JERUSALEM

Category: Yet Future.

This is one of the signs of the times in which many of our Christian friends also strongly believe. During the last days, before the Savior's Coming, two latter-day prophets will minister to the Jews in Jerusalem for a period of 42 months, that is, 3 1/2 years, after which time they will be killed. Their bodies will be left lying in the streets of Jerusalem for 3 1/2 days, during which people in Jerusalem and throughout the world will celebrate their deaths and will send gifts one to another as part of their celebration. After the 3 1/2 days have passed, the two prophets will be resurrected and the party will be "very over." It would be very difficult for those who know the scriptures to miss this sign of the times.

It is found in Revelation, chapter eleven. We will quote some of the verses here and bold some words and phrases for emphasis. But first, a note about a significant change made here by the Prophet Joseph Smith. In Revelation 11:3, it uses the phrase "two witnesses." This could mean any two people, including two missionaries or whoever. It reads as follows (bold added for emphasis):

> 3 And I will give *power* unto **my two witnesses**, and they shall prophesy a thousand two hundred *and* three-score days, clothed in sackcloth.

However, in D&C 77:15, Joseph Smith changed the word from "witnesses" to "prophets" as follows (bold added for emphasis):

> 15 Q. What is to be understood by the **two witnesses**, in the eleventh chapter of Revelation?
> A. **They are two prophets** that are to be raised up to the Jewish nation in the last days, at the time of the restoration, and to prophesy to the Jews after they are gathered and have built the city of Jerusalem in the land of their fathers.

Thus, we understand that these martyrs will necessarily be members of our First Presidency or of the Quorum of the Twelve Apostles. They are all sustained as "prophets, seers, and revelators" and as such are all prophets. One of my colleagues who was serving as a stake president at the same time I was told me that one of our Apostles mentioned this in a conversation with him. The Apostle told him that it was a very sobering thing to realize that two of them or their successors would fill this prophecy.

Quoting now from Revelation, chapter eleven, we will consider the following verses (bold added for emphasis plus explanatory notes in parentheses taken from *The New Testament Made Easier, Part 2*, by David J. Ridges, Cedar Fort Inc., 2003):

> 3 And I will give power unto my **two witnesses** (**two prophets** to the Jews in the last days; D&C 77:15), and they shall prophesy (serve, minister, prophesy, etc.) a thousand two hundred and threescore days (**1260 days, 42 months or 3 1/2 years**, about the same length as Christ's ministry), clothed in sackcloth (in humility).
>
> 4 These are the two olive trees (olive trees provide oil for lamps so people can be prepared to meet Christ; compare with the parable of the ten virgins in Matthew 25:1-13), and the two candlesticks (hold light so people can see clearly) standing before the God of the earth.
>
> 5 And if any man will hurt them (the two prophets), fire (the power of God to destroy) proceedeth out of their mouth, and devoureth their enemies (**the two prophets will be protected during their mission**): and if any man will hurt them, he must in this manner be killed (he will be killed by the power of God; Strong's #1163).
>
> 6 **These (two prophets) have power to shut heaven** (have the power of God; compare with the Prophet Nephi in Helaman 10:5-10 and 11:1-6), that it rain not in the days of their prophecy: and have power over waters to turn them to blood, and to smite the earth with all plagues (**to encourage people to repent**; to deliver from evil, bondage, as with the plagues in Egypt), as often as they will.
>
> 7 And **when they shall have finished their testimony** (ministry), the beast (Satan) that ascendeth out of the bottomless pit (Rev. 9:1-2) shall make war

against them (the two prophets), and shall overcome them, and **kill them**.

8 And **their dead bodies shall lie in the street** of the great city (Jerusalem), which spiritually is called Sodom and Egypt (i.e., is very wicked), where also our Lord was crucified.

9 And **they (the wicked)** of the people and kindreds and tongues and nations shall see their dead bodies three days and an half (perhaps symbolically tying in with their 3 1/2 year ministry as well as the Savior's three days in the tomb; the Savior was killed, too, by the wicked for trying to save them), **and shall not suffer (allow) their dead bodies to be put in graves** (many in eastern cultures believed that if the body is not buried, the spirit is bound to wander the earth in misery forever).

10 And **they that dwell upon the earth** (not just people in Jerusalem; implies that knowledge of the death of the two prophets will be widespread) **shall rejoice** over them, and **make merry**, and shall **send gifts one to another** (people all over the world will cheer and send gifts to one another **to celebrate** the deaths of these two prophets); because these two prophets tormented them (the wicked) that dwelt on the earth (implies that these prophets' influence was felt and irritated the wicked far beyond Jerusalem).

11 And **after three days and an half** the Spirit of life from God entered into them (**they are resurrected** at this time; see heading to chapter 11), and they stood upon their feet; and great fear fell upon them which saw them.

12 And they (the wicked who were celebrating) heard a great voice from heaven saying unto them (the two slain prophets), Come up hither. And **they ascended up to heaven** in a cloud; and their enemies beheld (saw) them.

13 And the same hour (immediately) was there a great earthquake, and the tenth part of the city fell, and in the earthquake were slain of men seven thousand: and the remnant were affrighted, and gave glory to the God of heaven (perhaps implying that **some of the wicked were converted** as was the case with the Savior's resurrection and also when Lazarus was brought back from the dead; if so, the deaths of the two prophets bore immediate fruit in helping some begin returning to God).

As mentioned above, this is a famous sign of the times, looked for by many good people in many different faiths. It will be one that the faithful will not miss.

48. THE MOUNT OF OLIVES WILL SPLIT IN TWO

Category: Yet Future.

In the last days, when the Jews are engaged in an unprecedented battle for survival as many wicked nations of the world lay siege to Jerusalem and the people of Judah, and it looks like they will be destroyed, the Savior will set foot on the Mount of Olives, just outside Jerusalem. It will split in two, and the remaining Jews will flee into the newly created rift in the mountain where they will meet their Savior. Elder Charles W. Penrose described this sign of the times as follows:

"His [Christ's] next appearance [after his appearance in the New Jerusalem] will be among the distressed and nearly vanquished sons of Judah. At the crisis of their fate, when the hostile troops of several nations are ravaging the city and all the horrors of war are overwhelming the people of Jerusalem, he will set his feet upon the Mount of Olives, which will cleave and part asunder at his touch. Attended by a host from heaven, he will overthrow and destroy the combined armies of

the Gentiles, and appear to the worshipping Jews as the mighty Deliverer and Conquerer so long expected by their race; and while love, gratitude, awe, and admiration swell their bosoms, the Deliverer will show them the tokens of his crucifixion and disclose himself as Jesus of Nazareth, whom they had reviled and whom their fathers put to death. Then will unbelief depart from their souls, and 'the blindness in part which has happened unto Israel' be removed." (Charles W. Penrose, "The Second Advent," Millennial Star, 10 Sept. 1859, p. 583.)

It is not likely that anyone who is familiar with the signs of the times will miss the fulfillment of this prophecy. The Doctrine and Covenants tells us that the whole world will feel the earthquake which is caused by the splitting of the Mount of Olives. In D&C 45:48 we read (bold added for emphasis):

> 48 And then shall the Lord set his foot upon **this mount**, and **it shall cleave in twain**, and **the earth shall tremble, and reel to and fro**, and **the heavens also shall shake**.

Another account of this great event is given in Zechariah 14:1-5 as follows (bold added for emphasis):

> 1 Behold, **the day of the LORD cometh**, and thy spoil shall be divided in the midst of thee.
>
> 2 For I will gather all **nations** (all the wicked) **against Jerusalem** to battle; and the city shall be taken, and the houses rifled, and the women ravished; and half of the city shall go forth into captivity, and the residue of the people shall not be cut off from the city.
>
> 3 **Then shall the LORD go forth, and fight against those nations**, as when he fought in the day of battle.
>
> 4 And **his feet shall stand in that day upon the mount of Olives**, which *is* before Jerusalem on the east, and **the mount of Olives shall cleave** in the

midst thereof toward the east and toward the west, *and there shall be* a very great valley; and half of the mountain shall remove toward the north, and half of it toward the south.

5 And **ye shall flee *to* the valley** of the mountains; for the valley of the mountains shall reach unto Azal: yea, ye shall flee, like as ye fled from before the earthquake in the days of Uzziah king of Judah: and **the LORD my God shall come, *and* all the saints with thee**.

Perhaps some day it will be reported on the news that a major earthquake has been recorded near Jerusalem and seismologists believe that it is the cause for the strange earthquake felt throughout the world. Furthermore, the news may well report that numerous Jews were seen fleeing into the valley caused by the earthquake. The faithful who are aware of the signs of the times will know what is going on and their testimonies will be strengthened. In fact, they will be excited to know that at that very moment the Savior is appearing to their fellow Israelites of the tribe of Judah and that a great conversion among the Jews is about to take place.

We now come to the final two signs of the times which we will consider in our list. These two will take place in the sequence given, whereas the other signs in our list of 50 have not necessarily been presented in chronological order.

49. THE RIGHTEOUS WILL BE TAKEN UP TO MEET THE COMING LORD AND THE WICKED WILL BE BURNED

Category: Yet Future.

When the time comes for the Savior to actually come, the righteous will be caught up to meet Him. We understand the "righteous" to mean those who are then living a celestial quality life. Many in the Christian world believe in this occurrence.

However, many of them are not sure whether it is literal or not. Many who believe it is literal expect that it will begin happening to the righteous some years before the actual Second Coming and that the worthy will gradually disappear until there are none but the wicked left on earth to be burned when He comes.

From modern revelation, we understand that it is indeed literal and that the righteous will be taken up as a group to meet the Master at the time of His coming. Since they will still be mortal, and since the Lord will come in full power and full glory, these saints will have to be "quickened" or "transfigured" in order to be in the presence of Christ without being burned by His glory. We also are told that these saints, along with the resurrected righteous, after they have been caught up to meet Him, will accompany Him as He descends to the earth to begin His millennial reign. These facts are summarized in D&C 88:96-98 as follows (bold added for emphasis):

> 96 And **the saints that are upon the earth, who are alive**, shall be **quickened** and be **caught up to meet him**.
>
> 97 And **they** (who are celestial quality) **who have slept in their graves shall come forth**, for their graves shall be opened; and they **also** shall be **caught up to meet him** in the midst of the pillar of heaven—
>
> 98 **They are Christ's**, the **first fruits** (celestial quality), they who **shall descend with him** first, and they who are on the earth and in their graves, who are first caught up to meet him; and all this by the voice of the sounding of the trump of the angel of God.

As stated above, it will be those who are living worthy of the celestial glory who are taken up, and those dead who are worthy of a celestial resurrection who rise from the grave and go up to meet Him. Those who are to be burned are those who are living a telestial lifestyle or a sons of perdition lifestyle. All this is found by reading D&C 88:96-102 as a block of related scripture. The question that remains in some people's minds is, "What happens to those who are living a terrestrial lifestyle at the time?" Answer. They will not be destroyed when the Savior comes, but we have no scriptural detail as to how they are preserved from being destroyed. We will have to wait for further revelation on this matter. In the meantime, Joseph Fielding Smith verified that it is celestials who will be caught up to meet Him. He said:

> "In modern revelation given to the Church, the Lord has made known more in relation to this glorious event. There shall be at least two classes which shall have the privilege of the resurrection at this time: First, those who 'shall dwell in the presence of God and his Christ forever and ever;' and second, honorable men, those who belong to the terrestrial kingdom as well as those of the celestial kingdom.

> "At the time of the coming of Christ, 'They who have slept in their graves shall come forth, for their graves shall be opened; and they also shall be caught up to meet him in the midst of the pillar of heaven-They are Christ's, the first fruits, they who shall descend with him first, and they who are on the earth and in their graves, who are first caught up to meet him; and all this by the voice of the sounding of the trump of the angel of God.' These are the just, 'whose names are written in heaven, where God and Christ are the judge of all. These are they who are just men made perfect through Jesus the mediator of the new covenant, who wrought out this perfect atonement through the shedding of his own blood.'" (Joseph Fielding Smith, Doctrines of Salvation, 3 vols., edited by Bruce R. McConkie [Salt Lake City: Bookcraft, 1954-1956], 2: 296.)

According to the Parable of the Wheat and the Tares, as given in D&C 86:7, the righteous will be taken up first, then the wicked will be burned. We read (bold added for emphasis):

> 7 Therefore, let the wheat and the tares grow together until the harvest is fully ripe; then ye shall **first gather out the wheat** from among the tares, and **after the gathering of the wheat, behold and lo, the tares are bound in bundles, and the field remaineth to be burned.**

As mentioned above, the wicked are those who are living a telestial lifestyle (see D&C 76:103 for a description) or the lifestyle of sons of perdition (see D&C 76:31-35 for a description of these.) They will be destroyed at the Second Coming. There are numerous scripture references to this effect. One of the most famous is Malachi 4:1 which is given here (bold added for emphasis):

> 1 For, behold, the day cometh, that shall burn as an oven; and all the proud, yea, and all that do wickedly, shall be stubble: and **the day that cometh shall burn them up**, saith the LORD of hosts, that it shall leave them neither root nor branch.

Many wonder how the wicked will be burned. There seem to be a number of opinions and theories about this. The scriptures, however, if carefully read, clearly say that the wicked will be burned by the glory of the coming Lord. Since they are not worthy to be "quickened" or transfigured with the righteous (see D&C 88:96), they will be consumed by the glory of Christ. Among other places in scripture, D&C 5:19 tell us (bold added for emphasis):

> 19 For a desolating scourge shall go forth among the inhabitants of the earth, and shall continue to be poured out from time to time, if they repent not, until the earth is empty, and the inhabitants thereof are consumed away and **utterly destroyed by the brightness of my coming.**

We read the same message in 2 Thessalonians 2:8 (bold added for emphasis):

8 And then shall that Wicked be revealed, whom the Lord shall consume with the spirit of his mouth, and **shall destroy with the brightness of his coming**:

Again, we read it in 2 Nephi 12:10, 19 and 21 (bold added for emphasis):

10 O ye wicked ones, enter into the rock, and hide thee in the dust, for the fear of the Lord and **the glory of his majesty shall smite thee**.

19 And they shall go into the holes of the rocks, and into the caves of the earth, for the fear of the Lord shall come upon them and **the glory of his majesty shall smite them**, when he ariseth to shake terribly the earth.

21 To go into the clefts of the rocks, and into the tops of the ragged rocks, for the fear of the Lord shall come upon them and **the majesty of his glory shall smite them**, when he ariseth to shake terribly the earth.

Since this will be a selective destruction, only those people and those things which do not belong on earth during the Millennium will be destroyed. This answers the concern which some people have who wonder if the temples will survive the burning at the Second Coming. Some have also wondered about the status of animals and other creatures when He comes. We understand that they are not judged, and that they will revert to the peaceful creatures they were before the fall of Adam. Thus, it appears that they will not be destroyed.

50. EVERYONE WILL SEE CHRIST WHEN HE COMES

Category: Yet Future.

In Revelation 1:7, we read that everyone will see the coming of the Savior, including those who caused His crucifixion. . (bold added for emphasis):

> 7 Behold, he cometh with clouds; and **every eye shall see him**, and **they** *also* **which pierced him**: and all kindreds of the earth shall wail because of him. Even so, Amen.

For some, this will be a wonderful day, for they will be transfigured and caught up to meet him (see D&C 88:96.) For others, it will be a time of great terror, for there is no escaping the accountability for their intentional wickedness. Speaking of the plight of the wicked at the Second Coming, Revelation 6:14–16 says (bold added for emphasis):

> 14 And the heaven departed as a scroll when it is rolled together; and every mountain and island were moved out of their places.
>
> 15 And (speaking of the wicked) **the kings of the earth, and the great men, and the rich men, and the chief captains, and the mighty men, and every bondman, and every free man, hid themselves** in the dens and in the rocks of the mountains;
>
> 16 And **said to the mountains and rocks, Fall on us, and hide us from the face of him that sitteth on the throne, and from the wrath of the Lamb**:

On the other hand, the righteous will have great cause to rejoice, for they will humbly greet the Savior and will be at peace in His presence. They will dwell with Him on earth as the Millennium begins. They will have the pleasure of associating with resurrected loved ones who visit the earth as needed to carry on with the work of the Lord. They will be in a society of true saints and others who will gradually accept the gospel and who will uphold righteousness on every side. They will enjoy the privilege of living at the time spoken of in scripture when (bold added for emphasis):

> 6 The wolf also shall dwell with the lamb, and the leopard shall lie down with the kid, and the calf and the young lion and fatling together; and a little child shall lead them.
>
> 7 And the cow and the bear shall feed; their young ones shall lie down together; and the lion shall eat straw like the ox.
>
> 8 And the sucking child shall play on the hole of the asp, and the weaned child shall put his hand on the cockatrice's den.
>
> 9 **They shall not hurt nor destroy in all my holy mountain, for the earth shall be full of the knowledge of the Lord, as the waters cover the sea.**

In summary, these and other signs of the times are strong and obvious witnesses that the gospel is true. They strengthen testimonies and assure that all the promises of the Lord will be fulfilled, including the wonderful promise that He will cleanse us from all sin if we come unto Him. The obvious fulfillment of these prophecies comes at a time in the history of the world when there is much of skepticism and unbelief in God. It is as if the Lord were saying that in the last days, He would provide such absolutely clear evidence that He exists that anyone who honestly considers these signs would have to conclude that the scriptures are true and therefore, there must be a God.

As stated at the beginning of this book, if we use these signs of the times as intended by the Savior, we will not use them to spread fear and panic. Rather we will adhere to the Master's counsel regarding them and not become troubled by them. We will use them to strengthen our knowledge that all His promises will be fulfilled. He told His disciples (bold added for emphasis):

Doctrine and Covenants 45:35.

> 35 And I said unto them: **Be not troubled**, for, when all these things shall come to pass, **ye may know** that the promises which have been made unto you shall be fulfilled.

CHAPTER 4

A COMPARISON OF CONDITIONS PRECEDING CHRIST'S APPEARANCE TO THE NEPHITES AND CONDITIONS LEADING TO THE SECOND COMING

There are many interesting parallels between the conditions among the Nephites, which led up to the coming of the resurrected Christ to them, and the conditions in our day which are leading up to the Second Coming of the Lord in our dispensation. We will note just a few of these parallels here. We will start in the Book of Helaman in the Book of Mormon. The timing at the beginning of Helaman is 85 years before the appearance of Jesus to the Nephites. Therefore, it is 85 years before the destruction of the wicked in the Americas and 85 years before the deliverance of the righteous from their wicked oppressors. The righteous Nephites and Lamanites in the Book of Mormon had 200 years of peace, whereas, the righteous who are spared at the Second Coming will be with Christ as the 1000 years of peace begin.

BOOK OF MORMON	OUR DAY
Helaman 1:1-13. Political turmoil and overthrow of governments, including political assassinations.	Same thing going on all over the world in our day.
Helaman 1:14; 3 Nephi 3:26. Wars and rumors of wars.	**D&C 45:26; Matt. 24:6.** Wars and rumors of wars.

Helaman 4:4. Many dissenters and apostates leave personal righteousness and join the enemies of the righteous.	Many dissenters abandoning the Bible and God's commandments and seeking to undermine laws and governments which strive to preserve righteous principles.
Helaman 4:12. Widespread personal wickedness and corruption.	Widespread personal wickedness and corruption.
Helaman 5:14–19. Great success in reactivating members, plus large numbers of converts to the Church.	Activation efforts are leading to increased activity and retention rates, plus large numbers of converts to the Church.
Helaman 6:12–14. Members of the Church prosper as a whole and have great joy and much revelation from God, in spite of such gross wickedness all around them.	Same thing happening among faithful members today.
Helaman 6:15–16. Increasing wickedness and more political assassinations.	Same thing happening throughout the world today.
Helaman 6:17. Materialism and pride take over the majority of society.	Same things happening throughout the world today.
Helaman 6:22–23. Secret combinations are formed to commit acts of terrorism against society.	Same things happening throughout the world today.
Helaman 6:31. The majority of society turns away from God and to wickedness.	Same things happening throughout the world today.

Helaman 6:35. The Spirit of the Lord begins to withdraw from the Nephites.	**D&C 63:32.** "I am holding my Spirit from the inhabitants of the earth."
Helaman 6:38. Government policies and laws are changed to support personal wickedness.	Laws are passed which support abortion, adultery, homosexuality, etc., remove God from public meetings, prohibit prayers in government and so on.
Helaman 7:4-6. Rapid take-over of government by unprincipled leaders who set aside God's commandments, etc.	Same things happening throughout the world today.
Helaman 11:1. Wars everywhere.	Same thing happening throughout the world today.
Helaman 11:4-6. People have ignored the gospel preaching, so famine is sent to humble them and reclaim as many as possible back to God.	**D&C 88:88-90.** Natural disasters happening throughout the world today for the same purpose.
Helaman 13:27-28. Many teach that there is no such thing as right and wrong. They gain popularity and large followings.	Same thing happening throughout the world today.
Helaman 14:6. Many signs and wonders in heaven.	**D&C 45:40.** Many signs and wonders in heaven and on the earth.
3 Nephi 1:22. Satan tries to get people to refuse to believe obvious signs and wonders.	**2 Peter 3:3-4.** Many people refuse to believe obvious signs and wonders in the last days.

3 Nephi 1:23. Much peace among faithful members of the Church.	Much peace and happiness among faithful members of the Church.
3 Nephi 2:14-16. Many Lamanites joined the Church.	**D&C 49:24.** Lamanites "blossom as the rose." Large numbers join the Church.
3 Nephi 3:9-10. The wicked claim that their evil works are good works.	Same things happening throughout the world today.
3 Nephi 6:11. Many lawyers were employed in the land.	Same things happening throughout the world today.
3 Nephi 7:2. Society divided up into ethnic groups who were against each other.	Same things happening throughout the world today.
3 Nephi 7:16. Nephi testified boldly to the people.	Church leaders today testify boldly to the world as well as to members.
3 Nephi 17-20. People got so wicked that they became angry at Nephi for doing miracles.	The wicked get very angry at the leaders of the Church as the Church continues its miraculous growth and service.
3 Nephi 7:22. Many miracles and great outpourings of the Spirit among the faithful.	The righteous today experience many miracles and great outpourings of the Spirit.
3 Nephi 7:26. Many baptisms just before the coming of the Lord (recorded in 3 Nephi 8.)	Convert baptisms continue to increase in unprecedented numbers.

CHAPTER 5

THE ACTUAL SECOND COMING OF CHRIST

Before we briefly consider what will happen at the time of the actual Second Coming, we will mention that there are some major appearances of Christ before the Second Coming which are often confused with His appearance to all the world. We will mention three of these comings here as follows, not necessarily in sequence:

1. To those in the New Jerusalem in America (3 Nephi 21:23-25; D&C 45:66-67.)

Before the Lord's Second Coming, the city of New Jerusalem will be built in Independence, Jackson County, Missouri. This "Holy City" (Moses 7:62) is often referred to as the "city of Zion" (D&C 57:2) and will continue on into the Millennium, serving as one of two capital cities for the Savior during the Millennium. The other capital city will be Old Jerusalem. The Savior will be in their midst.

2. To the Jews in Jerusalem (D&C 45:48; 51-53; Zechariah 12:10; 14:2-5)

When the Jews are being destroyed in an unprecedented siege against Jerusalem, they will be rescued by the appearance of the Savior upon the Mount of Olives. The Mount will split in two and the nearly vanquished Jews will flee into the valley that is formed. There, they will see the Savior and will ask Him to explain what happened to Him which caused such wounds in His hands and feet. He will then fight their battle for them and win.

3. To those assembled at Adam-Ondi-Ahman (Daniel 7:9-10, 13-14; D&C 116.)

"We now come to the least known and least understood thing connected with the Second Coming. . . It is a doctrine that has scarcely dawned on most of the Latter-Day Saints themselves;...Before the Lord Jesus descends openly. . . there is to be a secret appearance to selected members of His Church. He will come in private to his prophet and to the apostles then living. . . and further, all the faithful members of the church then living and all the faithful saints of all the ages past will be present. . . and it will take place in Davies County, Missouri, at a place called Adam-Ondi-Ahman. . . . The grand summation of the whole matter comes in these words: 'and also with all those whom my Father hath given me out of the world' (D&C 27:14). The sacrament is to be administered. . . this, of course, will be a part of the Grand Council at Adam-Ondi-Ahman." (From Bruce R. McConkie, *The Millennial Messiah*, pages 578-579 and 587.)

THE ACTUAL SECOND COMING

We will now briefly describe what will happen when the Savior actually comes to all the world. In order to keep it simple and to the point, we will present a few commonly asked questions associated with this long-awaited event and provide brief answers from the scriptures (bold added along with some explanatory notes in parentheses for teaching purposes).

QUESTION: What will happen to the faithful saints on the earth when He comes?
ANSWER: D&C 88:96.

96 And **the saints** that are **upon the earth, who are alive**, shall be **quickened** (transfigured) and be **caught up to meet him**.

QUESTION: Who is resurrected at His coming?
ANSWER: D&C 88:97.

97 And **they who have slept in their graves** (who are celestial quality) **shall come forth**, for their graves shall be opened; and **they also shall be caught up to meet him** in the midst of the pillar of heaven—

QUESTION: What color will He be wearing? Why will He wear that color?
ANSWER: D&C 133:46-51.

46 And it shall be said: Who is this that cometh down from God in heaven with dyed garments; yea, from the regions which are not known, clothed in his glorious apparel, traveling in the greatness of his strength?

47 And he shall say: I am he who spake in righteousness, mighty to save.

48 And the Lord shall be **red** in his apparel, and his garments like him that treadeth in the wine-vat.

49 And so great shall be the glory of his presence that the sun shall hide his face in shame, and the moon shall withhold its light, and the stars shall be hurled from their places.

50 And his voice shall be heard: I have trodden the wine-press alone, and have brought judgment upon all people; and none were with me;

51 And I have trampled them in my fury, and I did tread upon them in mine anger, and **their blood have I sprinkled upon my garments**, and stained all my raiment; for this was the day of vengeance (where the law of justice must be satisfied) which was in my heart.

QUESTION: From what direction will He Come?
ANSWER: Joseph Smith Matthew 1:26.

26 For as the light of the morning cometh **out of the east**, and shineth even unto the west, and covereth the whole earth, so shall also the coming of the Son of Man be.

QUESTION: How will the wicked be destroyed?
ANSWER: D&C 5:19.

19 For a desolating scourge shall go forth among the inhabitants of the earth, and shall continue to be poured out from time to time, if they repent not, until the earth is empty, and the inhabitants thereof are consumed away and **utterly destroyed by the brightness of my coming.**

QUESTION: What will happen to the earth?
ANSWER: D&C 133:23; Article of Faith 10.

D&C 133:23

23 He shall command the great deep, and it shall be driven back into the north countries, and **the islands shall become one land;**

Articles of Faith 10.

10 We believe in the literal gathering of Israel and in the restoration of the Ten Tribes; that Zion (the New Jerusalem) will be built upon the American continent; that Christ will reign personally upon the earth; and, that **the earth will be renewed and receive its paradisiacal glory.**

QUESTION: Who will actually come with Him?
ANSWER: D&C 88:98.

98 They are Christ's, **the first fruits** (those worthy of celestial glory), they who shall descend with him first, and **they who are on the earth and in their graves,** who are first caught up to meet him; and all this by the voice of the sounding of the trump of the angel of God.

QUESTION: Will everyone be caught off guard (like a "thief in the night")?
ANSWER: D&C 106:4-5.

4 And again, verily I say unto you, the coming of the Lord draweth nigh, and **it overtaketh the world** (the wicked and foolish) **as a thief in the night—**
5 Therefore, **gird up your loins** (be prepared with personal righteousness), **that you may be the children of light, and that day shall not overtake you as a thief.**

QUESTION: How will the wicked feel at this point?
ANSWER: Revelation 6:16.

16 And **said to the mountains and rocks, Fall on us, and hide us** from the face of him that sitteth on the throne, and from the wrath of the Lamb:

QUESTION: Will our prophets tell us the exact time of His coming?
ANSWER: Matthew 24:36.

36 But **of that day and hour knoweth no** *man,* no, not the angels of heaven, but my Father only.

QUESTION: Will things get better so the Savior can come?
ANSWER: D&C 84:97; 97:23.
Doctrine and Covenants 84:97

97 And **plagues shall go forth, and they shall not be taken from the earth** until I have completed my work, which shall be cut short in righteousness—

Doctrine and Covenants 97:23.

23 The Lord's scourge shall pass over by night and by day, and the report thereof shall vex all people; yea, **it shall not be stayed until the Lord come;**

QUESTION: As we see the "Signs of the Times" being fulfilled all around us, should we sort of PANIC?

ANSWER: Joseph Smith Matthew 1:23.

23 Behold, I speak these things unto you for the elect's sake; and you also shall hear of wars, and rumors of wars; **see that ye be not troubled**, for all I have told you must come to pass; but the end is not yet.

QUESTION: Who is resurrected when the Savior comes?

ANSWER: The righteous from Adam to Christ were resurrected with the Savior. D&C 133:54-55. **The righteous** who have died since then **will resurrect at the beginning of the Millennium**. D&C 88:97-98. **Next come those who lived terrestrial quality lives**, D&C 88:99, then at the end of the Millennium, telestials, D&C 88:101, and finally, sons of perdition, D&C 88:102.

CHAPTER 6
HOW GOOD DO YOU HAVE TO BE IN ORDER TO HAVE A PLEASANT SECOND COMING?

While we don't know if we will be around when the Second Coming takes place, nevertheless, the question posed as the title of this chapter is a very important one. Over many years of teaching and hearing students ask and answer this question in class discussions, it seems that a second question can be asked which will help lead to the answer to the first. The question is this: "In order to be in the presence of God, do you need to be **perfect**, or do you need to be **spotless**?"

Before we answer this second question, perhaps we should ask which of the following statements is correct:

1. No **imperfect** thing can dwell in the presence of God.

or

2. No **unclean** thing can dwell in the presence of God.

There are many scriptural references which will provide the correct answer for us, for instance (bold added for emphasis):

1 Nephi 10:21.

21 Wherefore, if ye have sought to do wickedly in the days of your probation, then ye are found unclean before the judgment-seat of God; and **no unclean thing can dwell with God**; wherefore, ye must be cast off forever.

Helaman 8:25.

> 25 But behold, ye have rejected the truth, and rebelled against your holy God; and even at this time, instead of laying up for yourselves treasures **in heaven**, where nothing doth corrupt, and **where nothing can come which is unclean,** ye are heaping up for yourselves wrath against the day of judgment.

3 Nephi 27:19.

> 19 And **no unclean thing can enter into his kingdom**; therefore nothing entereth into his rest save it be those who have washed their garments in my blood, because of their faith, and the repentance of all their sins, and their faithfulness unto the end.

The answer, repeated over and over again in the scriptures is that no **"unclean"** thing can return into the presence of God. In other words, we must be **spotless, not perfect**. This is very good news! It is summarized by Nephi as follows (bold added for emphasis):

2 Nephi 33:7.

> 7 I have charity for my people, and great faith in Christ that I shall meet **many souls spotless** at his judgment-seat.

If we get mixed up in our thinking between "spotless" and "perfect," and decide that we have to be perfect, it can lead to much discouragement and can lead some members to the point where they quit trying to live the gospel. With the help of the Savior and the Atonement, we can all get to the point where we can be made clean, or spotless, and thus qualify to enter back into the presence of God. Perfection will come along in due time after we have passed through the veil, but Christ was the only one who was perfect during mortality.

Elder Dallin H. Oaks of the Quorum of the Twelve Apostles gave some powerful advice, which helps us understand that we are not expected to become perfect in all things in this life. He said:

> "Another idea that is powerful to lift us from discouragement is that the work of the Church … is an eternal work. Not all problems … are fixed in mortality. The work of salvation goes on beyond the veil of death, and we should not be too apprehensive about incompleteness within the limits of mortality." (October 1995 General Conference.)

The Prophet Joseph Smith taught that there is much progress to be made after we pass through the veil. He said:

> "When you climb up a ladder, you must begin at the bottom, and ascend step by step, until you arrive at the top; and so it is with the principles of the Gospel—you must begin with the first, and go on until you learn all the principles of exaltation. But it will be a great while after you have passed through the veil before you will have learned them. It is not all to be comprehended in this world; it will be a great work to learn our salvation and exaltation even beyond the grave." (Joseph Smith, Teachings of the Prophet Joseph Smith, selected and arranged by Joseph Fielding Smith [Salt Lake City: Deseret Book Co., 1976], 348.)

Now, having been taught that we do not have to be perfect, rather, spotless, or clean, one major question remains, namely:

WHAT MUST WE DO TO ENABLE THE SAVIOR TO MAKE US CLEAN?

We could go on for some time giving many correct answers, including, "Keep the commandments." "Follow the Brethren." "Read the scriptures." "Say our prayers." "Serve one another." "Keep the Sabbath Day holy." And on and on. And each answer

would be correct as a part of a wonderful body of commandments and teachings designed to lead us back into the presence
of God. Since all faithful saints and all who desire to become
faithful are striving constantly to do these and many other good
things, there must be some simple, basic answer that provides
encouragement for the honest in heart, without being overwhelming. There must be some simple principle which gives us
confidence that we can qualify to have the Savior make us clean.
There is. It is found in Alma 34:33 and 36, as follows (bold added
for emphasis):

> 33 And now, as I said unto you before, as ye have had so
> many witnesses, therefore, I beseech of you that ye do
> not procrastinate the day of your repentance until the
> end; for after this day of life, which is given us to
> prepare for eternity, behold, if we do not **improve** our
> time while in this life, then cometh the night of dark-
> ness wherein there can be no labor performed.

> 36 And this I know, because the Lord hath said he
> dwelleth not in unholy temples, but in the hearts of the
> righteous doth he dwell; yea, and he has also said that
> **the righteous** shall sit down in his kingdom, to go no
> more out; but their garments should be **made white
> through the blood of the Lamb.**

The word "improve" in verse 33, above, becomes a key word.
If we "do not improve," we are in trouble. On the other hand, if
we do **improve**, sincerely, we enable the Savior to make us clean
through the Atonement (verse 36). Being made clean, we are
spotless. Being spotless, we are allowed to be in the presence of
God, where, as Joseph Smith pointed out in the previous quote,
we can continue to progress until we become perfect.

Elder Marvin J. Ashton of the Quorum of the Twelve
Apostles taught that the emphasis in the gospel of Christ is on
direction and diligence, not necessarily on speed. He taught the

importance of continuing improvement. In an address given in the April 1989 General Conference of the Church, he said:

"...the speed with which we head along the straight and narrow path isn't as important as the direction in which we are traveling."

IN SUMMARY:

How good do we have to be in order to have a pleasant Second Coming or Judgment Day? What will it take to be able to meet the Savior when we die?

Answer: We have to be honestly striving to be righteous. No matter where we are along the path which leads to the presence of the Father, if we want to be good, and we are sincerely improving, then we enable the Savior to make us clean. And thus, we can meet Christ and be welcomed into His presence.

ABOUT THE AUTHOR

David J. Ridges

David J. Ridges has been teaching for the Church Educational System for 35 years and has taught for several years at BYU Campus Education Week and Know Your Religion programs. He has also served as a curriculum writer for Sunday School, Seminary, and Institute of Religion manuals. He is also the author of the best-selling *Gospel Studies Series*, an in-depth study of the Standard Works of the LDS Church

He has served in many positions in the Church, including gospel doctrine teacher, bishop, stake president and patriarch.

Brother Ridges and his wife, Janette, are the parents of six children and make their home in Springville, Utah.

0   26575 77182   4